Let All the People Praise You

A Songbook

Northwestern Publishing House
Milwaukee, Wisconsin

Second printing, 2000

Northwestern Publishing House
1250 N. 113th St., Milwaukee, WI 53226-3284
© 1999 by Northwestern Publishing House.
Published 1999
Printed in the United States of America
ISBN 0-8100-0881-5 (bound)
ISBN 0-8100-0904-8 (spiral)

Introduction

When the first Lutheran hymnal was published in Germany in 1524, it contained only eight hymns. Four were by Martin Luther. A second hymnal, published several months later, contained 37 hymns, 24 by Luther. The great reformer took the lead in supplying hymns for the first Lutheran hymnals for three reasons: he wanted Christians to sing of Christ and his love, he wanted them to sing songs in which they confessed their faith in the teachings of the Bible, and he wanted to encourage poets and composers to produce more hymns for Christians to sing.

By God's grace and surely under his guidance, Martin Luther's pacesetting contributions in hymnody fostered a virtual outburst of congregational song in the Christian church. In the centuries since the Reformation, thousands of poets and composers, not only from the Lutheran church but also from other denominations, have written texts and crafted melodies that enable Christians to sing about Christ in a biblical and beautiful way. Wherever the gospel has been proclaimed and the Holy Spirit has brought people into the church, believers have experienced the faith-born desire to join their voices in Christ-centered songs. Poets and composers from many cultures and on every continent have produced hymns for Christians to sing.

When Christians sing hymns and spiritual songs that have roots in cultures and times other than their own, they put into practice their belief that God's people of all ages and places are members of one holy, apostolic, and universal church. As they walk through the weariness of life, Christians are strengthened not only by the peace that comes from the gospel and the joy they find in singing but also by the reality that millions of believers, on earth and in heaven, are one with them in faith and song.

Christian Worship: A Lutheran Hymnal, offered to the congregations of the Wisconsin Evangelical Lutheran Synod (WELS) in 1993, widened that denomination's hymn experiences and delighted many who were eager to sing a song of Christ in new and different styles. The committee that produced this hymnal felt strongly about including hymns and carols from many eras, nations, and cultures. In fact, the resolution that authorized *Christian Worship* instructed the committee to publish a hymnal that reflected "the larger perspective and mainstream of the worship of the Christian church." As stated in the hymnal's introduction, *Christian Worship* includes "in addition to Lutheran chorales and traditional English hymnody, a wide selection of plainsong hymns, spirituals, folk hymns from Appalachia, Wales, Ireland, and elsewhere, gospel hymns, and contemporary hymns in different styles."

While work was in progress on *Christian Worship,* the request to publish a book with additional songs was presented to the WELS Commission on Worship. Although the commission deemed such a book desirable, it recommended that actual publication be delayed until after the new hymnal was available. The subcommittee appointed to study the proposal reported its findings to the commission in 1991. The committee expressed the opinion that a definite need for such a songbook existed. Its report stated that "in schools it would provide a resource of music for junior choirs and classroom use beyond what the hymnal can supply. The songbook would also be usable in Sunday school and vacation Bible school programs where simpler music is sometimes desirable. Cross-cultural ministries would also welcome its use to provide music closer to the background of some ethnic groups, as well as easier music to introduce them to worship."

With the encouragement of the WELS Commission on Youth Discipleship and the Division of Home Missions, the Commission on Worship appointed a committee and authorized it to begin selecting songs for a book that would include some of these needed resources. Over the next several years, the committee went about the task of choosing appropriate texts and melodies. Serving on the committee were Carl Nolte (chairman), Mark Braun, Ned Goede, Mark Jeske, Daniel Koelpin, Michael Pfeifer, Mary Prange, and Leonard Proeber. The Commission on Worship reviewed the songs that were proposed, offered editorial suggestions, deleted a few selections, and authorized publication.

Let All the People Praise You is not intended to be a replacement for *Christian Worship: A Lutheran Hymnal.* For that reason, it includes no orders of worship, prayers, or songs found in that hymnal. A hymnal unites a church body as a worshiping community and allows its many congregations and members to confirm their confessional unity by means of hymns and songs they share and sing together. The hymnal is wisely the preeminent and primary resource in the worship life of every congregation. *Let All the People Praise You* will be useful where leaders and people feel a need in their specialized ministries for more of the kind of songs and hymns that the hymnal offers only in limited quantity.

All of the texts included in *Let All the People Praise You* have been carefully reviewed for doctrinal content. Changes were made in several texts to express biblical truth more completely. Obviously, not all songs will match the doctrinal precision of the Lutheran Confessions. It is in the nature of poetry to express biblical truth in imagery and metaphor, not only in doctrinal language. Not every song in *Let All the People Praise You* is intended for public worship, but each song does sing of Christ in its own way. Every song, as the Spirit carries out his work, may lead a person closer to Christ's love and give someone else a vehicle with which to praise Christ's holy name.

Martin Luther's statement that "next to the Word of God, music deserves the highest praise" is often quoted. The observation comes from Luther's preface to a 1538 German hymnal. He goes on to speak about the benefits of singing: "For whether you wish to comfort the sad, to terrify the happy, to encourage the despairing, to humble the proud, to calm the passionate, or to appease those full of hate . . . what more effective means than music could you find?" (*Luther's Works,* American Edition, Vol. 53, p. 323). May this songbook prove itself spiritually beneficial to the people of God as they make music in their hearts to the Lord (Ephesians 5:19).

Victor H. Prange, chairman
WELS Commission on Worship

Alabaré

Note: "Alabaré a mi Señor" means "I will praise my Lord."

Verse

1. Wor - thy is Christ,— the Lamb who was slain,— Whose
2. John saw the num - ber of all those re - deemed,— And
1. *Dig - no es Cris - to, el cor - de - ro inmo - lado; Su*
2. *Juan vió el núm - ero de los re - di - mi - dos, Y*

blood— set us free from our— sins.—
all were sing - ing prais - es to the Lord.—
sang - re nos li - bró— de nuestros pecados.—
to - dos al - a - ba - ban al Se - ñor.—

Pow - er and rich - es and wis - dom and strength— And
Thou - sands were pray - ing, ten thou - sands re - joic - ing, And
Pod - er y ri - que - zas y sab - iduría y forta - leza Y
U - nos or - a - ban, y ot - ros can - ta - ban Y

hon - or and all bless - ing shall be his.
all were sing - ing prais - es to the Lord.
hon - or— y ben - dición sean a él.
tod - os a - la - ba - ban al Se - ñor.

Text and Tune: Manuel José Alonso and José Pagán.

Firmes y adelante
(Onward, Christian Soldiers)

1. ¡Firmes y adelante, huestes de la fe,
   Sin temor alguno, que Jesús nos ve!
   Jefe soberano, Cristo alfrente va,
   Y la regia enseña tremolando está.

   Refrain
   ¡Firmes y adelante, huestes de la fe,
   Sin temor alguno, que Jesús nos ve!

2. Tronos y coronas pueden perecer;
   De Jesús la iglesia fiel habrá de ser;
   Nada encontra suya prevalecerá,
   Porque la promesa nunca faltará.

   Refrain

3. ¡Muévete potente, pueblo del Señor!
   Y de triunfo en triunfo marcha con valor.
   Eres sólo un cuerpo, y uno es el Señor,
   Una la esperanza y uno nuestro amor.

   Refrain

Text: Arthur S. Sullivan, English; Juan Bautista Cabrera, Spanish tr.

All Night, All Day

Refrain

All night, all day, an-gels watch-in' o-ver me, my Lord.— All night, all day, an-gels watch-in' o-ver me.———

Verse

1. Day is dy-in' in— the west; An-gels watch-in' o-ver me, my
2. Now I lay me down— to sleep; An-gels watch-in' o-ver me, my
3. Lord, stay with me through— the night; An-gels watch-in' o-ver me, my

Lord.— Sleep, my child, and take—your rest; An-gels watch-in' o-ver me.
Lord.— Pray the Lord my soul— to keep; An-gels watch-in' o-ver me.
Lord.— Wake me with the morn-ing light; An-gels watch-in' o-ver me.

Text, Tune, Setting: African-American spiritual.

All Things Bright and Beautiful

lit - tle bird— that sings, He— made their glow - ing—
riv - er run - ning by, The— sun - set, and the—
pleas - ant sum - mer sun, The— ripe fruits in the—
lips— that we— might tell How— great is God Al -

col - ors, He— made their ti - ny— wings.
morn - ing That— bright - ens up the— sky.
gar - den, He— made them, ev - 'ry— one.
might - y, Who— has made all things— well.

Oh, qué amigo nos es Cristo
(What a Friend We Have in Jesus)

1. ¡Oh, qué amigo nos es Cristo!
   Él llevó nuestro dolor,
   Y nos manda que llevemos
   Todo a Dios en oración.
   ¿Vive el hombre desprovisto
   De paz, gozo y santo amor?
   Esto es porque no llevamos
   Todo a Dios en oración.

2. ¿Vives débil y cargado
   De cuidados y temor?
   A Jesús, refugio eterno,
   Dile todo en oración.
   ¿Te desprecian tus amigos?
   Dilo a Cristo en oración;
   En sus brazos gozo tierno
   Hallará tu corazón.

3. Jesucristo es nuestro amigo;
   De esto pruebas Él nos dió
   Al sufrir el cruel castigo
   Que el culpable mereció.
   Y su pueblo redimido
   Hallará seguridad
   Fiando en este amigo eterno
   Y esperando en su bondad.

Text: Joseph M. Scriven, alt.; tr. C. Garza Mora.

Alleluia

Alleluia to Jesus

1. As Ja - cob with trav - el was wea - ry one day,— At— night on a stone— for a pil - low he lay; He— saw in a vi - sion a lad - der so high That its
2. This lad - der is long,— it is strong and well-made,— Has stood hun - dreds of years— and is not yet de-cayed; Ma - ny mil - lions have climbed it and reached Zi - on's hill, And—
3. Come, let us as - cend, for— such is God's will;— For the an - gels of Ja - cob are guard - ing it still. And re - mem - ber, each step that by faith we pass o'er, Some—
4. And when we ar - rive— at the land of the blest,— We shall hear the glad words, "Come to heav - en - ly rest. Here are re - gions of light, here are man - sions of bliss." Oh,—

foot was on earth___ and its top in the sky:
thou - sands by faith___ are___ climb - ing it still:
proph - et or mar - tyr has climbed it be - fore:
who would not climb___ such a lad - der as this?

Al - le - lu - ia to Je - sus, who died on the tree___ And has

raised up a lad - der of mer - cy for me, And has

raised up a lad - der of mer - cy for me.

Text: English folk song. Tune: JACOB'S LADDER. Setting: Carl Schalk.
Setting: from *All God's People Sing* © 1978 Concordia Publishing House. Used by permission.

The Angel Rolled the Stone Away

1. Sis - ter Mar - y, she came run - ning_____ Just a - bout the
2. Said the an - gel, "He is not here;_____ He is ris - en
3. Je - sus said, "Don't hold me, Mar - y,_____ But go on a -
4. Broth - er Thom - as, he came run - ning,_____ And his eyes were

break of day._____ She was bring - ing news from heav - en_____
as he said._____ Why— do you seek the liv - ing—
head of me._____ Go and tell all my dis - ci - ples—
o - pen wide._____ Je - sus said, "Man, if you doubt me,—

____ That the an - gel rolled the stone a - way._____
____ 'Way— down— here a - mong the dead?"_____
____ To— meet— me in Gal - i - lee."_____
____ Come,- put your hand right in my side."_____

As the Deer

1. As the deer pants— for the wa - ter, So my
2. You're my friend, and— you're my bro - ther, E - ven

soul longs af - ter you. You a - lone are my
though you are a King. I love you more than

heart's de - sire,— And I long to wor - ship you.
an - y oth - er, So much more than an - y - thing.

Text, Tune, Setting: Martin Nystrom.

The Battle Belongs to the Lord

1. In____ heav-en-ly ar - mor we'll en - ter the land;____ The
2. When the pow-er of dark-ness comes in____ like a flood,____ The
3. When your en-e-my press-es in hard,____ do not fear;____ The

bat - tle be - longs____ to the Lord.____ No
bat - tle be - longs____ to the Lord.____ He'll
bat - tle be - longs____ to the Lord.____ Take

weap-on that's fash - ioned a-gainst____ us will stand;____ The
raise up a stand - ard, the pow'r____ of his blood;____ The
cour-age, my friend,____ your re-demp - tion is near;____ The

bat - tle be - longs___ to the Lord.___
bat - tle be - longs___ to the Lord.___
bat - tle be - longs___ to the Lord.___ And we sing glo - ry,

hon - or, pow - er, and strength___ to the Lord!___ We sing

glo - ry, hon - or, pow - er, and strength___ to the Lord!___

Text, Tune, Setting: Jamie Owens-Collins.
Setting: © 1984 and this arrangement © 1990 Fairhill Music. Used by permission.

Be Thou My Vision

1. Be thou my vision, O Lord of my heart;
2. Be thou my breast-plate, my sword for the fight;
3. Rich-es I need not, nor man's emp-ty praise;
4. High King of heav-en, my vic-to-ry won,

Naught be all else to me, save that thou art.
Thou my whole ar-mor and thou my true might;
Thou mine in-her-i-tance now and al-ways;
May I reach heav-en's joys, O bright heav'n's Sun.

Thou my best thought in the day and the night;
Thou my soul's shel-ter and thou my strong tow-er.
Thou and thou on-ly the first in my heart;
Heart of my own heart, what-ev-er be-fall,

Wak - ing and sleep - ing, thy__ pres - ence my light.
Raise thou me heav'n - ward, great__ Pow'r of my pow'r.
High King of heav - en, my__ treas - ure thou art.
Still be my vi - sion, O__ Rul - er of all.

Text: Ancient Irish; tr. Mary E. Byrne; versified Eleanor H. Hull. Tune: SLANE.
Setting: ©1982 Concordia Publishing House. Used by permission.

Before the Marvel of This Night

peace,   That fear and death and sor - row   cease: Sing
bliss,   A teas - ing taste of what they   miss: Sing
love   That rules our u - ni - verse a - bove: Sing

peace, sing peace, sing gift of peace,_____ Sing peace, sing
bliss, sing bliss, sing end - less bliss,_____ Sing bliss, sing
love, sing love, sing God is love,_____ Sing love, sing

1., 2.

gift of peace!_____
end - less bliss!_____
God is love!_____

3.

Behold What Manner of Love

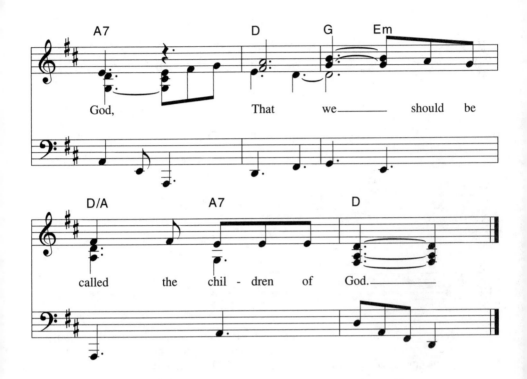

God, That we should be called the chil - dren of God.

Beside Your Manger Here I Stand

1. Be - side— your man - ger here I stand, Child— Je - sus, my dear— Sav - ior. I bring— you gifts with will - ing hands, All— to - kens of your—

2. When in— the night of grief I lay, Lord— Je - sus, you con - soled— me. You brought— to me the light of day; Your— an - gels still en -

3. I beg— of you, Christ Child di - vine, Oh,— grant me this great— fa - vor: That you— may be for - ev - er mine And— ev - er be my—

Text: Klug, *Geistliche Lieder auffs new gebessert*, Wittenberg; tr. Walter E. Buszin, st. 1,3. Tune: ES IST GEWISSLICH.
Setting: J. S. Bach.
Text: tr. from *101 Chorales* © 1952 Hall & McCreary Company. Used by permission.

Blessed Assurance

1. Bless - ed as - sur - ance, Je - sus is mine!___ Oh, what a
2. Joy - ful con - fes - sion, I am his own!___ Fol - low - ing
3. Lov - ing sub - mis - sion, all is at rest;___ I in my

fore - taste of glo - ry di - vine!___ Heir of sal - va - tion, pur - chase of
Je - sus, I'm nev - er a - lone.___ Born of his Spir - it, I am re -
Sav - ior am hap - py and blest,___ Watch - ing and wait - ing, look - ing a -

God,___ Born of his Spir - it, washed in his blood.___
stored,___ Strength - ened to serve my Sav - ior and Lord.___
bove,___ Filled with his good - ness, kept in his love.___

This is my sto - ry, this is my song,___ Prais - ing my Sav - ior all the day long;___ This is my sto - ry, this is my song,___ Prais - ing my Sav - ior all the day long.___

Text: Fanny J. Crosby, st. 1,3; Marie J. Post, st. 2. Tune: Phoebe P. Knapp.

Blessing

Oh, may the peace of God be with you ev-er-more, And may the pow'r of his great love your soul a-gain___ re-store, And may you al-ways know his nev-er-end-ing___ care And feel his gra-cious Spir-it up-on you ev-'ry-where.

Text, Tune, Setting: Natalie Sleeth. Setting adapt. Carl Nolte.
Text, Tune, Setting: © 1974 Choristers Guild. Used by permission.

Blest Be the Tie That Binds

1. Blest be__ the tie__ that binds Our hearts__ in
2. Be - fore__ our Fa - ther's throne We pour__ our
3. We share__ our mu - tual woes, Our mu - tual
4. From sor - row, toil,__ and pain And sin__ we

Chris - tian love; The fel - low - ship__ of
ar - dent prayers; Our fears,__ our hopes,__ our
bur - dens bear, And of - ten for__ each
shall__ be free And per - fect love__ and

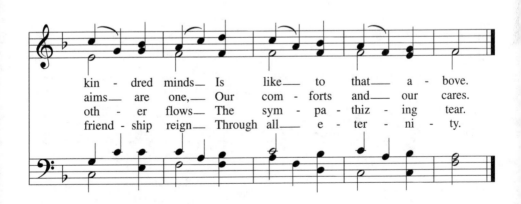

kin - dred minds__ Is like__ to that__ a - bove.
aims__ are one,__ Our com - forts and__ our cares.
oth - er flows__ The sym - pa - thiz - ing tear.
friend - ship reign__ Through all__ e - ter - ni - ty.

Text: John Fawcett. Tune (DENNIS): Johann G. Nägeli, adapt. Setting: Lowell Mason.

The Blood Will Never Lose Its Power

1. The

blood that Je - sus shed for me
soothes my doubts— and calms my fears,

Way back on Cal - va - ry, The
And it dries all my tears. The

blood that gives me strength from day to day,— It will
blood that gives me strength from day to day,— It will

nev - er lose its pow'r.
nev - er lose its pow'r.

It reach-es— to the high - est moun - tain;

It flows to the low - est val - ley.

The blood that gives me strength from day to

day, It will nev - er lose its

pow'r.   2. It   pow'r.   Oh,   it will

nev - er   lose   its   pow'r.———

Borning Cry

35

2. I was there when you were but a child, With a
4. If you find some-one to share your time And you
6. When the eve - ning gent-ly clos-es in And you

faith to suit you well; In a blaze of light you
join your hearts as one, I'll be there to make your
shut your wea-ry eyes, I'll be there as I have

wan-dered off To find where de-mons dwell.
vers-es rhyme From dusk till ris-ing sun.
al-ways been With just one more sur-prise.

Text, Tune (WATERLIFE), Setting: John Ylvisaker.
Text, Tune, Setting: © 1985 John Ylvisaker, Box 321, Waverly IA 50677. Used by permission.

Breath of the Living God
(Soplo de Dios)

1. Breath of the liv-ing God on the wa-ters in the be-gin-ning
2. Breath of the liv-ing God, you con-ceived the Son, Je-sus, to be
3. Breath of the liv-ing God, you bring us to life in bap-tis-mal

mov - ing, Breath of the liv-ing God, you fill all cre-
like___ us; Breath of the liv-ing God, so you re - cre-
wa - ter; Breath of the liv-ing God, we new crea-tures

a - tion with fruit-ful life.
ate all who live in him. Come now and live with-in___ us,
live by your liv-ing breath.

and with your gifts en - rich___ us, Breath of the liv-ing

God, O most ho - ly Spir - it___ of the Lord!

1. Soplo de Dios viviente que en
   El principio cubriste el agua;
   Soplo de Dios viviente que
   Fecundaste la creación.
   ¡Ven hoy a nuestras almas,
   Infúndenos tus dones,

   Refrain
   Soplo de Dios viviente,
   Oh Santo Espíritu del Señor!

2. Soplo de Dios viviente por
   Quien el hijo se hizo hombre,
   Soplo de Dios viviente que
   Renovaste la creación.
   ¡Ven hoy a nuestras almas,
   Infúndenos tus dones,

   Refrain

3. Soplo de Dios viviente por
   Quien nacemos en el bautismo;
   Soplo de Dios viviente que
   Consagraste la creación.
   ¡Ven hoy a nuestras almas,
   Infúndenos tus dones,

   Refrain

Change My Heart, O God

Change my heart, O God;— make it ev-er true.—

— Change my heart, O God;—

may I be like you. you.—

You are the pot - ter;

I am the clay.___ Mold me and

make___ me, this is what I pray.

D.C. al Fine

Text, Tune, Setting: Eddie Espinosa.

Christ Is Risen

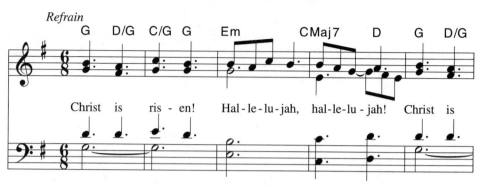

Refrain

Christ is ris - en! Hal - le - lu - jah, hal - le - lu - jah! Christ is

ris - en, ris - en in - deed! Hal - le - lu - jah!

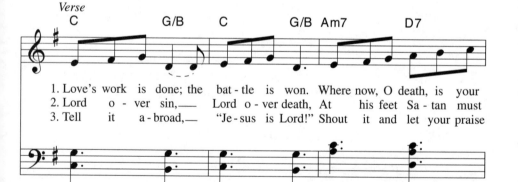

Verse

1. Love's work is done; the bat - tle is won. Where now, O death, is your
2. Lord o - ver sin,— Lord o - ver death, At his feet Sa - tan must
3. Tell it a - broad,— "Je - sus is Lord!" Shout it and let your praise

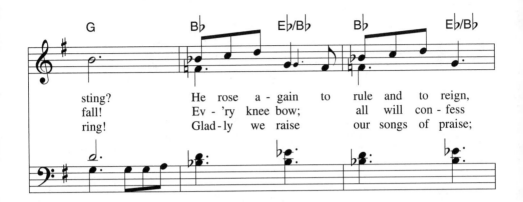

sting?   He rose a - gain to rule and to reign,
fall!   Ev - 'ry knee bow; all will con - fess
ring!   Glad - ly we raise our songs of praise;

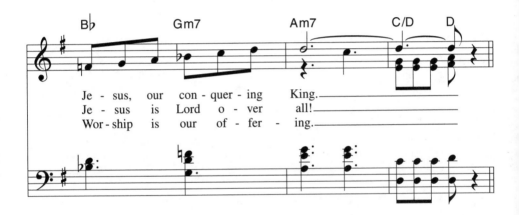

Je - sus, our con - quer - ing King.
Je - sus is Lord o - ver all!
Wor - ship is our of - fer - ing.

Text, Tune, Setting: Chris Rolinson.
Text, Tune, Setting: © 1989 Thankyou Music. Used by permission.

Christ, Mighty Savior

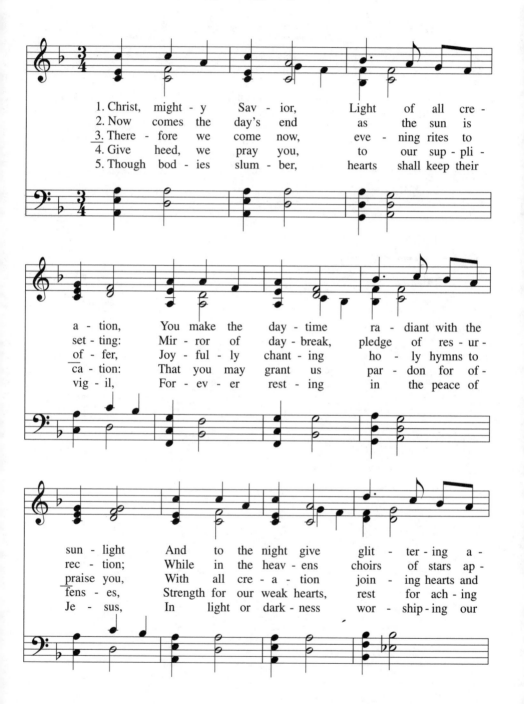

1. Christ, might - y Sav - ior, Light of all cre - a - tion, You make the day - time ra - diant with the sun - light And to the night give glit - ter - ing a -

2. Now comes the day's end as the sun is set - ting: Mir - ror of day - break, pledge of res - ur - rec - tion; While in the heav - ens choirs of stars ap -

3. There - fore we come now, eve - ning rites to of - fer, Joy - ful - ly chant - ing ho - ly hymns to praise you, With all cre - a - tion join - ing hearts and

4. Give heed, we pray you, to our sup - pli - ca - tion: That you may grant us par - don for of - fens - es, Strength for our weak hearts, rest for ach - ing

5. Though bod - ies slum - ber, hearts shall keep their vig - il, For - ev - er rest - ing in the peace of Je - sus, In light or dark - ness wor - ship - ing our

dorn - ment,	Stars_____	in	the	heav	-	ens.
pear - ing	Hal -	low	the	night	-	fall.
voic - es	Sing -	ing	your	glo	-	ry.
bod - ies,	Sooth -	ing	the	wea	-	ry.
Sav - ior	Now_____	and	for -	ev	-	er.

Text: Mozarabic Rite; tr. Alan G. McDougall; rev. tr. Anne K. LeCroy. Tune (MIGHTY SAVIOR) and Setting: David Hurd.
Text: tr. used by permission of Anne K. LeCroy. Tune and Setting: © 1985 GIA Publications. Used by permission.

Christ Is the King

1. Christ is the King! O friends, re - joice; Broth-ers and sis-ters,
2. Oh, mag - ni - fy the Lord, and— raise An - thems of joy and
3. O Chris-tian wo - men, Chris-tian— men, All the world o - ver,

with— one voice Give glo - ry to the Fa - ther's Choice.
ho - ly praise For all his saints of an - cient days.
seek— a - gain The way his faith - ful fol-lowed then.

Al - le - lu - ia, al - le - lu - ia, al - le - lu - ia!
Al - le - lu - ia, al - le - lu - ia, al - le - lu - ia!
Al - le - lu - ia, al - le - lu - ia, al - le - lu - ia!

Text: George K. A. Baell, alt. Tune (BEVERLY): Charles R. Anders.
Text: used by permission of Oxford University Press. Tune and Setting: © 1978 *Lutheran Book of Worship*. Used by permission of Augsburg Fortress.

Clap Your Hands

1. Clap your hands, all you peo-ple. Shout un-to God with a voice of tri-umph!

2. Clap your hands, all you peo-ple. Shout un-to God with a voice of praise! Ho-

3. san - na! Ho - san - na! Shout un-to God with a voice of tri-umph!

4. Praise him! Praise him! Shout un-to God with a voice of praise!

Text and Tune: Jimmy Owens. Setting: Dale Grotenhuis.
Text, Tune, Setting: © 1972 Bud John Songs. Used by permission of EMI.

The Coloring Song

1. Red is the col-or of the blood that flowed Down the
2. Blue is the col-or of a heart so cold, That___
3. Gold is the col-or of the morn - ing sun That___
4. Brown is the col-or of the au - tumn leaves When the

face of some - one who loved us so. He's the
will not bend when the sto - ry's told Of the
shines so free - ly on ev - 'ry - one. It's the
win - ter comes to the bar - ren trees. There is

per - fect___ Man;___ he's the Lord's own Son; He's the
love of___ God___ for a sin - ful race, Of the
sun a - bove___ that___ keeps us warm; It's the
birth, there is death,___ there___ is a plan, And there's

Come and Praise the Lord

Lord, For his mer-cy is won-drous in our eyes.

won-drous in our eyes.

Text: Steffi G. Rubin. Tune and Setting: Stuart Dauermann.
Text, Tune, Setting: © 1982 Lillenas Publishing Co. (administered by The Copyright Company, Nashville TN). All rights reserved. International Copyright Secured.
Used by permission.

Come, Let Us Eat

Our Lord's bod - y, let us take to - geth - er.
Je - sus' blood poured, let us drink to - geth - er.
In the pres - ence of our Lord we gath - er.
Je - sus, ris - en, will bring in the king - dom.

Text: Billema Kwillia, st. 1-3; tr. Margaret D. Miller, alt.; Gilbert E. Doan, st. 4. Tune: Billema Kwillia. Setting: Leland Sateren.

Come, Praise the Lord

53

Tune: traditional. Setting: Larry Mayfield.

The Coventry Carol

1. Lul - ly lul - lay, thou lit - tle ti - ny child, bye - bye, lul - ly lul - lay.

2. O sis - ters, too, how may we do
3. Her - od the king in his rag - ing
4. Then woe is me, my child, for thee!
5. Child, do not stay, do not de - lay;

For to pre - serve this day This poor young -
Charg - ed he hath this day His men of
And ev - 'ry morn and day For thy part -
To E - gypt haste, a - way! For thy re -

ling   for whom we   sing   Bye - bye,   lul - ly lul   -   lay?
might in   his   own   sight   All   young chil - dren to   slay.
ing   nor   say   nor   sing   Bye - bye,   lul - ly lul   -   lay.
turn   thy   folk shall yearn,   Bye - bye,   lul - ly lul   -   lay.

6. Lul - ly lul - lay, thou lit - tle ti - ny child, bye - bye, lul - ly lul - lay.

Text: Robert Croo, st. 1-4,6; Mark A. Jeske, st. 5. Tune: traditional English. Setting: Martin Shaw.
Text, st. 5: © 1996 Mark A. Jeske. Used by permission. Setting: used by permission of Oxford University Press.

Daughter of Zion

1. Daugh - ter of Zi - on, shout_____ for joy!
2. Hail, ho - san - na, Da - vid's Son!
3. Hail, ho - san - na, Da - vid's Son!

Shout_____ a - loud, Je - ru - sa - lem!
See_____ your peo - ple's palms_____ of praise.
Hear_____ our wel - come, gra - cious King!

Christ_____ your King_____ now__ comes to you;
Your_____ e - ter - nal king - dom__ come!
Firm - ly stands your throne__ of__ peace,

See,_____ he comes, the Prince_____ of peace.
Praise_____ be sung to God_____ on high!
God_____ the Fa - ther's on - ly Son!

Daugh - ter of Zi - on, shout⸻ for joy!
Hail, ho - san - na, Da - vid's Son!
Hail, ho - san - na, Da - vid's Son!

Shout⸻ a - loud, Je - ru - sa - lem!
See⸻ your peo - ple's palms⸻ of praise.
Hear⸻ our wel - come, gra - cious King!

Text: Joh. J. Eschenburg; tr. H. Brueckner; alt. Mark A. Jeske. Tune (JUDAS MACCABEUS) and Setting: George F. Handel.

Stille Nacht
(Silent Night)

1. Stille Nacht, heilige Nacht!
   Alles schläft, einsam wacht
   *Nur das traute hochheilige Paar.
   Holder Knabe im lockigen Haar;
   Schlaf' in himmlischer Ruh!
   Schlaf' in himmlischer Ruh!

2. Stille Nacht, heilige Nacht!
   Hirten erst kundgemacht;
   Durch der Engel Halleluja
   Tönt es laut von fern und nah:
   Christ, der Retter, ist da!
   Christ, der Retter, ist da!

3. Stille Nacht, heilige Nacht!
   Gottes Sohn, o wie lacht
   Lieb' aus deinem göttlichen Mund,
   Da uns schläget die rettende Stund',
   Christ, in deiner Geburt!
   Christ, in deiner Geburt!

*Variant German version for lines three to six
of stanza 1:

Nur das heilige Elternpaar,
Das im Stalle zu Bethlehem war
Bei dem himmlischen Kind,
Bei dem himmlischen Kind.

Text: Franz Joseph Mohr.

Deep River

Text and Tune: African-American spiritual. Setting: Mark A. Jeske.
Setting: © 1995 Mark A. Jeske. Used by permission.

Didn't My Lord Deliver Daniel

fi - 'ry fur - nace, And why not ev - er - y man?

2. The wind blows east, and the wind blows west; It
3. He set my foot on the gos - pel ship, And the
4. The moon run down in a pur - ple stream; The
5. Oh, Dan - iel cast in the li - on's den, He

blows like the judg - ment— day. And ev - 'ry poor soul— that
ship it be - gin— to— sail. It land - ed me o - ver on
sun for - bear— to— shine. And ev - er - y star— did
pray both— night— and— day. The an - gel came— from

ev - er did pray Will be— glad— to pray— that day.
Ca - naan's shore,— And I'll nev - er come— back an - y - more.
dis - ap - pear.— King— Je - sus— shall— be mine.
Gal - i - lee— And— took— that— li - on a - way!

Text and Tune: African-American spiritual. Setting: Carl Haywood.
Setting: from *The Haywood Collection of Negro Spirituals* © 1992 Walton Music Corp. Used by permission.

Do, Lord

1. Do, Lord, oh, do, Lord, Do re-mem-ber___ me.
2. When I'm in trou-ble, Do re-mem-ber___ me.
3. When I am dy-ing, Do re-mem-ber___ me.
4. When this world's on fire, Do re-mem-ber___ me.

Do, Lord, oh, do, Lord, Do re-mem-ber___ me.
When I'm in trou-ble, Do re-mem-ber___ me.
When I am dy-ing, Do re-mem-ber___ me.
When this world's on fire, Do re-mem-ber___ me.

Do, Lord, oh, do, Lord, Do re-mem-ber___
When I'm in trou-ble, Do re-mem-ber___
When I am dy-ing, Do re-mem-ber___
When this world's on fire, Do re-mem-ber___

me. Oh, do, Lord, re - mem - ber me.
me. Oh, do, Lord, re - mem - ber me.
me. Oh, do, Lord, re - mem - ber me.
me. Oh, do, Lord, re - mem - ber me.

Text and Tune: African-American spiritual. Setting: Mark A. Jeske.

El Shaddai

64

El Shaddai — melody line with lyrics:

Bb / EbMaj7 / C *last time to Coda*

We will praise_ and lift you high,_ El Shad-dai._

F Fsus4 F Gm

1. Through your love_ and through the ram,_
2. Through the years_ you made it clear_

C C/E F Bb

— you saved the son_ of A-bra-ham._ Through the pow-
— that the time_ of Christ_ was near,_ Though the peo-

EbMaj7 A/C# A Dm C/E

- er of_ your hand, you turned the sea_ in-to_ dry land._
- ple could_ not see_ what Mes-si-ah ought_ to be._

66

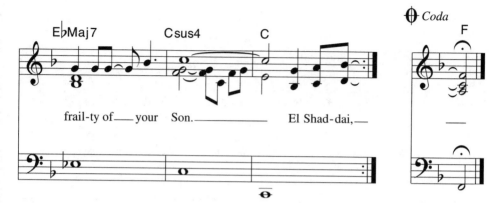

frail-ty of___ your Son._____ El Shad-dai,___

Text: Michael J. Card. Tune and Setting: John W. Thompson.

Eternal Light

1. E - ter - nal Light, shine in my heart;
2. E - ter - nal Life, raise me from death;
3. Un - til by your most cost - ly grace,

E - ter - nal Hope, lift up my eyes;
E - ter - nal Bright - ness, help me see;
In - vit - ed by your ho - ly Word,

E - ter - nal Pow'r, be my sup - port;
E - ter - nal Spir - it, give me breath;
At last I come be - fore your face

E - ter - nal Wis - dom, make me wise.
E - ter - nal Sav - ior, come to me.
To know you, my e - ter - nal God.

Father, I Adore You

1. Fa - ther, I a - dore you, lay my life be -
2. Je - sus, I a - dore you, lay my life be -
3. Spir - it, I a - dore you, lay my life be -

fore you. How I love you!
fore you. How I love you!
fore you. How I love you!

Father Welcomes

Refrain

Fa - ther wel - comes all— his chil - dren

To— his fam - 'ly through his Son. Fa - ther giv - ing

his— sal - va - tion; Life— for - ev - er has been won.

Verse

1. Lit - tle chil - dren, come— to me,
2. In the wa - ter, in— the Word,
3. Let us dai - ly die— to sin;

For my king - dom is of these.
In his prom - ise, be as - sured;
Let us dai - ly rise with him,

Love and new life have I to give,
All who be - lieve and are bap - tized
Walk in the love of Christ our Lord,

Par - don for your sin.
Have been born a - gain.
Live in the peace of God.

Text, Tune, Setting: Robin Mann.
Text, Tune, Setting: © Kevin Mayhew. Used by permission. License No. 898021.

Jesus Loves Me
(Spanish translation)

Cristo me ama, bien lo sé,
Su palabra me hace ver.
Que los niños son de Aquel.
Quien es nuestro Amigo fiel.

Refrain
¡Cristo me ama!
¡Cristo me ama!
¡Cristo me ama!
La Biblia dice así.

Pronunciation:
Creesto may ahma, bee-ehn lo say,
Soo pahlahbra may ahsay vayr.
Kay los neenyos sohn day Ahkayl.
Keyen ays nooaystro Ahmeego fee-el.

Refrain
¡Creesto may ahma!
¡Creesto may ahma!
¡Creesto may ahma!
La Beebleea deesay ahsee.

The First Song of Isaiah

va - tion. And on that day you shall say "Give thanks to the
joy,———————— for the great one—— in the midst of—

to Refrain

Lord!" and call up - on his—— name.—————
you is the Ho - ly—— One of—— Is - rael.———

Sav - ior. 2. Make his deeds known a - mong the peo - ples;

see that they re - mem - ber that his name is ex - alt - ed.——

Sing the prais-es of the Lord, for he has done great things, and this is known in all the world.

to Refrain

Coda

Sav-ior. Sure-ly, it is God who saves me; I will trust in him and not be a-fraid. For the Lord is my strong-hold and my sure de-fense, and he will be my Sav-ior.

For Since Christ's Feet

1. For since Christ's feet in an - cient times Walked up-on
2. Wor - thy the Lamb who once was slain, Wor - thy is
3. Oh, sing for joy and shout with praise! Ex - ult in

earth in right-eous-ness, And since the ho - ly Lamb of
Christ, who rose on high. To him all hon - or, pow'r, and
him, O all the earth! Bring him your mind, your strength, your

God Was slain to end our wretch - ed - ness, We have God's
praise, And glo - ry lift - ed to the sky. Praise to our
love, And sing to all his sav - ing worth! We'll nev - er

stead - fast love di - vine Now point - ing out the
gra - cious God and Lord, Whose Spir - it now to
cease from serv - ing him Nor let his sword sleep

heav'n - ly way, And there's a new Je - ru - sa -
us de - scends To breathe new life in life - less
in our hand Un - til we see Je - ru - sa -

lem A - wait - ing the tri - um - phant day!
souls And grant the joy that nev - er ends.
lem De - scend - ing from the heav'n - ly land.

Text: David Prillwitz and Stanley Stein; rev. Mark Braun. Tune (JERUSALEM): Charles H. Parry.
Text: © 1984 David Prillwitz and Stanley Stein. Used by permission.

Friends

1. Pack-ing up___ the dreams___ God plant-ed
2. With the faith___ and love___ God's giv-en

in the fer - tile soil___ of you;___
spring-ing from___ the hope___ we know,___

can't be - lieve___ the hopes___ he's grant-ed means a
we will pray___ the joy___ you'll live in

chap-ter in___ your life___ is through.___ But we'll keep you close___
is the strength___ that now___ you show.___ But we'll keep you close___

Jesus Loves Me
(Chinese translation)

Yea Sue eye woh, woh jer dau,
Ihn way Shung Jing gau sue woh.
Fahn shau hi dz Jew Moo Yang.
Woh swaye rahn ruoh Tah chi-ang jwang.

Refrain
Jew Yea Sue eye woh!
Jew Yea Sue eye woh!
Jew Yea Sue eye woh!
Ihn Shung Jing gau sue woh.

Pronunciation:
The above is an English version of the
Chinese pronunciation.

Translation by Kevin Stellick. Used by permission.

From Him All Blessings Flow

1. Be - hind the storm, the howl - ing wind, and light - ning flash - es
2. In an - y storm that life may bring, when winds of trou - ble

bright, A smil - ing coun - te - nance is there to
blow, A grace and love will see you through; from

guard you through the night. A smil - ing coun - te -
him all bless - ings flow. A grace and love will

nance is there to guard you through the night.—
see you through; from him all bless-ings flow.—

So let his

love shine in—— through-out the dark-est night!— Oh, let his love shine

in! Oh, let it shine!——

Text, Tune, Setting: Robert A. Roesch.

Gathered 'Round Your Table

1. Gath - ered 'round your ta - ble We re - joice and grieve,
2. Prince of glo - ry, grac - ing Heav'n ere time be - gan,
3. Laid in man - ger yon - der, Giv - en for our sake—
4. Beth - l'em's in - car - na - tion, Cal - v'ry's bit - ter cross,

View - ing Beth - l'em's sta - ble On that ho - ly eve;
Now for us em - brac - ing Death as Son of man,
With pro - found - est won - der We your bod - y take;
Worked for us sal - va - tion By your pain and loss.

Joy to see you ly - ing In your man - ger bed,
By your birth so low - ly, By your love so true,
Hushed in ad - o - ra - tion We ap - proach the cup,
Now we kneel be - fore you In this ho - ly place;

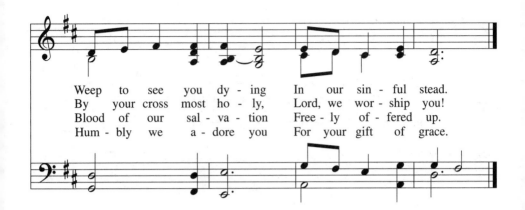

Weep to see you dy - ing   In our sin - ful stead.
By your cross most ho - ly,   Lord, we wor - ship you!
Blood of our sal - va - tion   Free - ly of - fered up.
Hum - bly we a - dore you   For your gift of grace.

Text: Edith Margaret Clarkson. Tune (GREENRIDGE) and Setting: Tom Fettke.

Give Thanks

85

done for— us. And now let the weak say "I am
strong," let the poor say "I am rich" be-cause of

second time to Coda ✛   D.C. al Coda

what the Lord has done for— us.

✛ *Coda*

thanks.

us. Give thanks. Give thanks. Give thanks.—

Glorify Thy Name

1. Fa - ther, we love you; we wor - ship and a - dore you,
2. Je - sus, we love you; we wor - ship and a - dore you,
3. Spir - it, we love you; we wor - ship and a - dore you,

Glo - ri - fy thy name in all the earth.
Glo - ri - fy thy name in all the earth.
Glo - ri - fy thy name in all the earth.

Glo - ri - fy thy name, glo - ri - fy thy name,
Glo - ri - fy thy name, glo - ri - fy thy name,
Glo - ri - fy thy name, glo - ri - fy thy name,

glo - ri - fy thy name in all the earth.
glo - ri - fy thy name in all the earth.
glo - ri - fy thy name in all the earth.

Text, Tune, Setting: Donna Adkins.

Go

Go Down, Moses

1. When Is - rael was in E - gypt's land, Let my peo - ple
2. "Thus saith the Lord," bold Mo - ses said, Let my peo - ple
3. The Lord told Mo - ses what to do, Let my peo - ple
4. Oh, let us all from bond - age flee, Let my peo - ple

go, Op - pressed so hard they could not stand, Let my peo - ple go.
go, "If not, I'll smite your first - born dead," Let my peo - ple go.
go, To lead the He - brew chil - dren through, Let my peo - ple go.
go, And let us all in Christ be free, Let my peo - ple go.

Go down, Mo - ses, Way down in E - gypt's land; —

Tell — old — Phar - aoh, Let my peo - ple go.

Text and Tune: African-American spiritual. Setting: John W. Work.

Go into the World

Text, Tune, Setting: Natalie Sleeth.
Text, Tune, Setting: © 1979 Choristers Guild. Used by permission.

God Be in My Head

God be in my head and in my un-der-stand-ing; God be in my eyes and in my look-ing; God be in my mouth and in my speak-ing; God be in my heart and in my think-ing; God be at my death and at my de-part-ing.

Text: from a French *Horae Diurnae B.V.M.*, as adapted in Pynson's *Sarum Primer*. Tune (DAVID) and Setting: George W. Briggs.
Tune and Setting: by permission of Oxford University Press.

God Loves Me Dearly

1. God loves me dear - ly, grants me sal -
2. I was in bond - age, sin, death, and
3. He sent forth Je - sus, my dear Re -
4. Je - sus, my Sav - ior, him - self did

va - tion; God loves me dear - ly, loves e - ven me.
dark - ness; God's love was work - ing to make me free.
deem - er; He sent forth Je - sus and set me free.
of - fer; Je - sus, my Sav - ior, paid all I owed.

There - fore I'll say a - gain: God loves me dear - ly, God loves me

dear - ly, loves e - ven me.

Text: August Rische; tr. composite. Tune: GOTT IST DIE LIEBE.

God Rest You Merry, Gentlemen

1. God rest you mer - ry, gen - tle - men, Let
2. From God our heav'n - ly Fa - ther A
3. The shep - herds at those ti - dings Re -
4. But when to Beth - le - hem they came, Where -

noth - ing you dis - may, For Je - sus Christ our
bless - ed an - gel came, And un - to cer - tain
joic - ed much in mind, And left their flocks a -
at this in - fant lay, They found him in a

Sav - ior Was born up - on this day, To
shep - herds Brought ti - dings of the same, How
feed - ing In tem - pest, storm, and wind, And
man - ger, Where ox - en feed on hay; His

save us all from Sa - tan's
that in Beth - le - hem was
went to Beth - le - hem straight -
moth - er, Mar - y, kneel -

pow'r When we were gone a - stray:
born The Son of God by name:
way This bless - ed babe to find:
ing, Un - to the Lord did pray:

Oh,— ti - dings of com - fort and joy, com - fort and

joy, Oh,— ti - dings of com - fort and joy.

Text and Tune: English carol. Setting: John Stainer.

God, Whose Giving Knows No Ending

1. God, whose giv - ing knows no end - ing From your
2. Skills and time are ours for press - ing Toward the
3. Treas - ure too you have en - trust - ed, Gain through

rich and end - less store: Na - ture's won - der, Je - sus'
goals of Christ, your Son: All at peace in health and
pow'rs your grace con - ferred; Ours to use for home and

wis - dom, Cost - ly cross, grave's shat - tered
free - dom, Rac - es joined, the church made
kin - dred And to spread the gos - pel

door. Gift - ed by you, we turn to you, Of - f'ring
one. Now di - rect our dai - ly la - bor Lest we
Word. O - pen wide our hands in shar - ing As we

up   our - selves— in praise;   Thank - ful   song   shall   rise for -
strive for   self—   a - lone;   Born   with   tal - ents,   make us
heed Christ's age - less call,   Heal - ing, teach - ing,   and re -

ev - er,   Gra - cious   Do - nor   of   our   days.
ser - vants   Fit   to   an - swer   at   your   throne.
claim - ing,   Ser - ving   you   by   lov - ing   all.

God Will Take Care of You

1. Be not dis - mayed___ what - e'er be - tide,
2. Through days of toil when your heart may fail,
3. All you may need___ he will pro - vide,

God will take care of you;___ Be - neath his wings___ of
God will take care of you;___ When dan - gers fierce___ your
God will take care of you;___ Noth - ing you ask___ will

love a - bide, God will take care of you.___
path as - sail, God will take care of you.___
be de - nied, God will take care of you.___

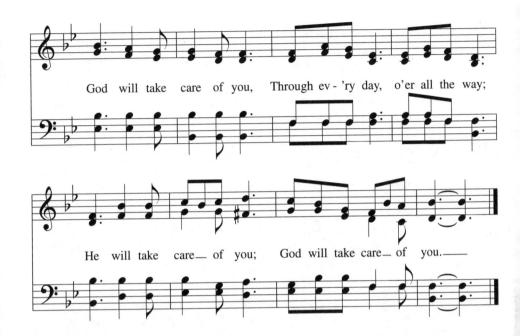

God will take care of you, Through ev - 'ry day, o'er all the way;

He will take care— of you; God will take care— of you.——

Text: Civilla D. Martin, alt. Tune: W. Stillman Martin.

Great Is the Lord

Great is the Lord; he is ho-ly and just; By his pow-er we trust in his love._____

Great is the Lord; he is faith-ful and true; By his mer-cy he proves he is love._____

1., 2. Great is the Lord and
3. Great are you, Lord, and

wor-thy of glo-ry! Great is the Lord and wor-thy of praise.
wor-thy of glo-ry! Great are you, Lord, and wor-thy of praise.

Great is the Lord; now lift up your voice, now lift up your voice:
Great are you, Lord; I lift up my voice, I lift up my voice:

Great_____ is the Lord!_____ Great_____
Great_____ are you, Lord!_____ Great_____

1., 3.
_____ is the Lord!_____
_____ are you, Lord!_____

2.
Lord!

D.S.

Text, Tune, Setting: Michael W. Smith and Deborah D. Smith.
Text, Tune, Setting: © 1982 Meadowgreen Music Co. Used by permission of EMI.

He Is Born, the Child Divine

Refrain

He is born, the— child di - vine; Play the—
o - boe,— sound the bag - pipes. He is born, the—
child di - vine; Sing, ye all, he is born to - day.

Verse

1. Proph - ets from the— a - ges past Have fore -
2. Ah, how fair is the ho - ly child, And how
3. In a man - ger— was he born; Straw, a
4. King of all for - ev - er - more, Lit - tle

told the— Sav - ior's com - ing; We for more than four
per - fect— are his grac - es; Ah, how fair is the
lit - tle,— for his cra - dle. In a man - ger—
in - fant— though thou art,— King of all for -

thou - sand years Have a - wait - ed this joy - ous time.
ho - ly child; Oh, how sweet is the child di - vine.
was he born; What a lodg - ing for Christ the Lord!
ev - er - more, Reign in ev - 'ry— hu - man heart.

Text and Tune: traditional French carol. Setting: Walter Ehret.
Setting: from *The International Book of Christmas Carols* © 1963, 1980 Walter Ehret and George K. Evans. Used by permission.

He Is Exalted

ev - er his truth shall reign.___ Heav - en and

earth re - joice in his ho - ly name.___

He is ex - alt-ed; the King is ex - alt - ed on high.___

He Is the Way, He Is the Truth, He Is the Life

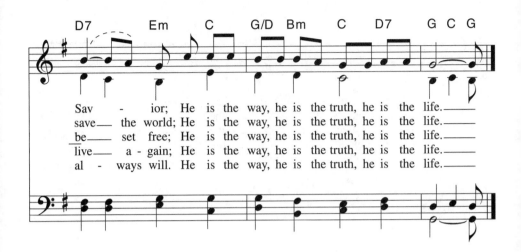

Sav - ior; He is the way, he is the truth, he is the life.____
save__ the world; He is the way, he is the truth, he is the life.____
be__ set free; He is the way, he is the truth, he is the life.____
live__ a - gain; He is the way, he is the truth, he is the life.____
al - ways will. He is the way, he is the truth, he is the life.____

Text, Tune, Setting: Otis Skillings.

He Never Said a Mumbalin' Word

1. They crucified— my Lord, And he
2. They nailed him to— the tree, And he
3. They pierced him in— the side, And he
4. The blood came trick - a - lin' down, And he
5. He hung his head— and died, And he

nev - er said a mumb - a - lin' word; They crucified— my
nev - er said a mumb - a - lin' word; They nailed him to— the
nev - er said a mumb - a - lin' word; They pierced him in— the
nev - er said a mumb - a - lin' word; The blood came trick - a - lin'
nev - er said a mumb - a - lin' word; He hung his head— and

Lord, And he nev - er said a mumb - a - lin'
tree, And he nev - er said a mumb - a - lin'
side, And he nev - er said a mumb - a - lin'
down, And he nev - er said a mumb - a - lin'
died, And he nev - er said a mumb - a - lin'

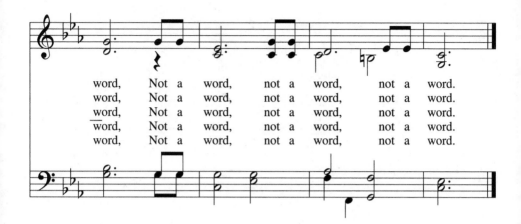

word,   Not   a   word,   not   a   word,   not   a   word.
word,   Not   a   word,   not   a   word,   not   a   word.
word,   Not   a   word,   not   a   word,   not   a   word.
word,   Not   a   word,   not   a   word,   not   a   word.
word,   Not   a   word,   not   a   word,   not   a   word.

Text, Tune, Setting: African-American spiritual.

He Walks among the Golden Lamps

1. He walks a-mong the gold — en lamps On feet like bur-nished bronze: His hair as snows of win-ter white, His eyes with fire a-flame, and bright His glo — rious robe of seam-less light, Sur-pass-ing Sol - o - mon's.

2. And in his hand the sev — en stars, And from his mouth a sword: His voice the thun-der of the seas; All crea-tures bow to his de-crees Who holds the ev - er-last-ing keys And reigns as sov-'reign Lord.

3. More ra-diant than the sun at noon, Who was and is to be: Who was from ev - er-last-ing days; lives, the Lord of all our ways— To him be maj-es-ty and praise For all e-ter-ni - ty.

Text: Timothy Dudley-Smith. Tune (REVELATION) and Setting: Robert LeBlanc.

He's Got the Whole World in His Hands

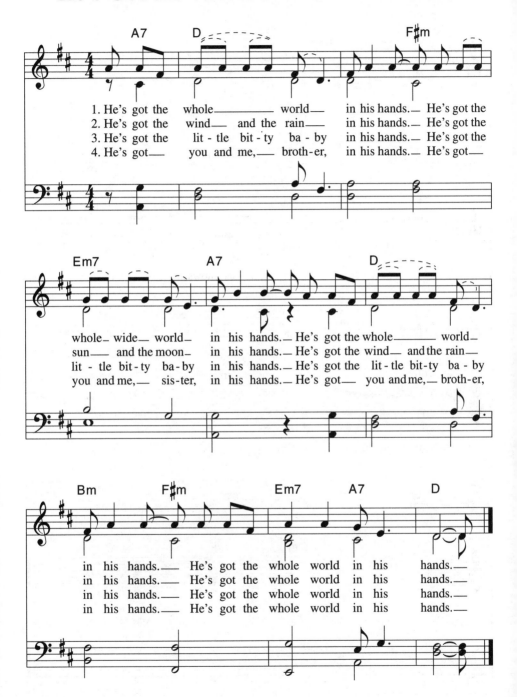

1. He's got the whole_____ world___ in his hands.__ He's got the
2. He's got the wind__ and the rain___ in his hands.__ He's got the
3. He's got the lit - tle bit - ty ba - by in his hands.__ He's got the
4. He's got__ you and me,__ broth - er, in his hands.__ He's got__

whole__ wide__ world__ in his hands.__ He's got the whole_____ world__
sun__ and the moon__ in his hands.__ He's got the wind__ and the rain__
lit - tle bit - ty ba - by in his hands.__ He's got the lit - tle bit - ty ba - by
you and me, __ sis - ter, in his hands.__ He's got__ you and me, __ broth - er,

in his hands.__ He's got the whole world in his hands.__
in his hands.__ He's got the whole world in his hands.__
in his hands.__ He's got the whole world in his hands.__
in his hands.__ He's got the whole world in his hands.__

Text, Tune, Setting: African-American spiritual.

Here He Comes

1. Je - sus said, "I'll come back for you."
2. Hap - py day when the Lord comes back.

Drop your trou - bles; lift your eyes.
Clap your hands in jub - i - lee.

Heav - en's door will be o - pened up as
"You are mine," says the Lord of love, "so

glo - ry lights up the skies.
come to my home with me."

Text, Tune, Setting: David Morstad.
Text, Tune, Setting: © 1989 David Morstad, Watertown WI. Used by permission.

His Eye Is on the Sparrow

1. Why should I feel dis-cour-aged?___ Why should the shad-ows
2. "Let not your heart be trou-bled,"___ His ten-der word I
3. When-ev-er I am tempt-ed,___ When-ev-er clouds a-

come?___ Why should my heart be lone-ly___
hear,___ And rest-ing on his good-ness,___
rise,___ When songs give place to sigh-ing,___

And long for heav'n and home___ When Je-sus is___ my
I lose my doubt and fear;___ Though by the path___ he
When hope with-in me dies,___ I draw the clos-er

por - tion?——— My con - stant friend—— is he:——— His
lead - eth,——— But one step I—— may see:——— His
to him;——— From care he sets—— me free:——— His

eye is on—— the spar-row,——— And I know he watch - es
eye is on—— the spar-row,——— And I know he watch - es
eye is on—— the spar-row,——— And I know he cares for

me;——— His eye is on the spar-row,——— And I
me;——— His eye is on the spar-row,——— And I
me;——— His eye is on the spar-row,——— And I

116

know he watch-es me._____
know he watch-es me._____ I sing be-cause I'm
know he cares for me._____

hap-py;_____ I sing be-cause I'm free,_____ For his

eye is on the spar-row,___ And I know he watch-es me._____

Text: Civilla D. Martin. Tune (SPARROW): Charles H. Gabriel.

Jesus Loves Me
(German translation)

Jesus liebt mich ganz gewiss,
Denn die Bibel sagt mir dies.
Alle Kinder schwach und klein
Lad't er herzlich zu sich ein.

Refrain
Ja, Jesus liebt mich!
Ja, Jesus liebt mich!
Ja, Jesus liebt mich!
Die Bibel sagt mir dies.

Pronunciation:
Yay-soos leebt mik gahnts geh-viss,
Denn dee Bee-behl zahgt meer dees.
Ah-leh Keen-dehr shvahk oont kline
Lahd ehr hehrt-slik tsoo zich ine.

Refrain
Yah, Yay-soos leebt mik!
Yah, Yay-soos leebt mik!
Yah, Yay-soos leebt mik!
Dee Bee-behl zahgt meer dees.

His Name Is Wonderful

His name is Won-der-ful, His name is Won-der-ful,

His name is Won-der-ful, Je-sus, my Lord.

He is the might-y King, Mas-ter of ev-'ry-thing;

His name is Won-der-ful, Je-sus, my Lord.

He's the great Shep-herd, The Rock of all a - ges,

Al - might - y God is he.

Bow down be - fore him; Love and a - dore him.

His name is Won - der - ful, Je - sus, my Lord.

Text, Tune, Setting: Audrey Mieir.

Holy, Holy, Holy
(Santo, Santo, Santo)

"Ho - ly, ho - ly, ho - ly," an - gel hosts are sing - ing.
"San - to, san - to, san - to," can - tan se - ra - fi - nes.

"Ho - ly, ho - ly, ho - ly is the Lord our God.
"San - to, san - to, san - to, Dios es el Se - ñor.

Ho - ly, ho - ly, ho - ly is God, the Lord of might. Your
San - to, san - to, san - to, es fuer - te nue - stro Dios. Tu

glo - ry fills the heav - ens; your glo - ry fills the earth." Ho -
glo - ria lle - na los cie - los; la tie - rra lle - na es - tá." *Ho -*

san - na in the high - est, ho - san - na is our song.
sa - na en las al - tu - ras, ho - sa - na la can - ción.

Text: English para. Bert Polman. Tune: traditional Spanish. Setting: AnnaMae Meyer Bush.
Text and Setting: © 1987 CRC Publications. Used by permission.

How Excellent Is Your Name

mid - night blue____ and see the work__ you've done.__
trum - pets play____ and the dead in Christ__ shall rise,__

Your chil - dren raise__ a per - fect praise__ while
The cho - sen few__ will gath - er to__ pro -

en - e - mies hold__ their tongue. Cre - a - tion shows__ your
claim__ you Lord__ Most High. With joy - ful al - le -

splen - dor, your reign - ing maj - es -
lu - ias the heav - en - ly host__ will__

ty,   And   yet   I   find you   take   the   time   to
sing.   Ev - 'ry   knee shall   bow and   tongue will shout, "You

care   for   one   like   me!
are   the   King   of   kings."   How

Text, Tune, Setting: Dick Tunney, Melodie Tunney, and Paul Smith.
Text, Tune, Setting: © 1985 Laurel Press/Pamela Kay Music, Marquis III Music, and Word Music. Used by permission.

How Majestic Is Your Name

O   Lord,   our Lord,   how ma - jes - tic is your

name in all   the   earth! O   earth! O

Lord, we praise your name. O
Lord, we mag - ni - fy your name:— Prince of
peace, might - y God, O Lord God Al -
might - y. O y.

1. D.S. 2.

I Am Thine, O Lord

1. I am thine, O Lord; I have heard thy voice, And it
2. Con - se - crate me now to thy ser - vice, Lord, By the
3. Oh, the pure de - light of a sin - gle hour That be -
4. There are depths of love that I can - not know Till I

told thy love to__ me. But I long to rise in the
pow'r of grace di - vine; Let my soul look up with a
fore thy throne I__ spend; When I kneel in prayer, and with
cross the nar - row__ sea; There are heights of joy that I

arms of faith And be clos - er drawn to thee.
stead - fast hope And my will be lost in thine.
thee, my God, I com - mune as friend with friend!
may not reach Till I rest in peace with thee.

Draw me near - er, near - er, bless - ed Lord, To the cross where thou hast died; Draw me near - er, near - er, near - er, bless - ed Lord, To thy pre - cious, bleed - ing side.

Text: Fanny J. Crosby. Tune and Setting: W. H. Doane.

I Bind unto Myself Today

I bind un - to my - self to - day The
strong name of the Trin - i - ty By
in - vo - ca - tion of the same, The
Three in One and One in Three.

130

Text: attr. St. Patrick; para. Cecil F. Alexander. Tune: traditional Irish.
Setting: © 1969 Concordia Publishing House. Used by permission.

Jesus Loves Me
(Apache translation)

1. Jesus áń zhą́ bił nshǫǫ,
   Binaltsoos shił nagoldi',
   Chągháshé dawa bíyéé
   Doo daanłdzil da, bíí nalwod

   Refrain
   Jesus bił nshooníí
   Jesus bił nshooníí
   Jesus bił nshooníí
   Binaltsoos shił nagoldi'.

2. Jesus dayúweh bił nshǫǫ,
   Doo niłdzil da shą' ndi,
   Áń shinchǫ' yits'ą' shíłteeh
   Tsįhíí yiká' shá dastsąą.

   Refrain

3. Jesus áń zhą́ shá dastsąą,
   Yaaká' zhį́ shá ch'íńtąą.
   Áń shinchǫ' dawa naił'eeł,
   Bizhaazhé yude' owa.

   Refrain

4. Jesus áń zhą́ bił nshǫǫ,
   Dahayú bił aanásht'ash.
   Áń bidił shá idezjool,
   Áń zhą́ bee hinshdaa doleeł.

   Refrain

Pronunciation guide:
   a = *a* as in *father*
   e = *e* as in *bed*
   i = *i* as in *bid*
   o = *o* as in *low*
   u = *u* as in *use*
   ˎ = nasal sound
   ´ = high nasal tone
   ' = glottal stop (stop short)

Translation by Edgar Perry. Used by permission.

I Don't Feel No Ways Tired

I don't feel no ways tired._____ I come too

far from where I start - ed from.____ No - bod - y

told me that the road would be eas - y;____ I

don't be - lieve he brought me this far to leave me.____

I Lift My Eyes to the Quiet Hills

1. I lift my eyes to the qui - et hills In the press of a bu - sy day; As green hills stand in a dus - ty land, So

2. I lift my eyes to the qui - et hills To a calm that is mine to share, Se - cure and still in the Fa - ther's will And

3. I lift my eyes to the qui - et hills With a prayer as I turn to sleep; By day, by night, through the dark and light, My

4. I lift my eyes to the qui - et hills And my heart to the Fa - ther's throne; In all my ways to the end of days The

God_____ is my strength and stay.
kept_____ by the Fa - ther's care.
Shep - herd will guard his sheep.
Lord_____ will pre - serve his own.

I Love You, Lord

I love you, Lord, _____ and I lift my voice _____ to wor-ship you; O my soul, re-joice. Take joy, my King, _____ in _____ what you hear; _____ may it be a sweet, sweet _____ sound in _____ your ear. _____

I Need Thee Every Hour

1. I need thee ev-'ry hour, Most gra - cious Lord;
2. I need thee ev-'ry hour; Stay thou near - by.
3. I need thee ev-'ry hour In joy or pain;
4. I need thee ev-'ry hour; Teach me thy will,

No ten - der voice like thine Can peace af - ford.
Temp - ta - tions lose their pow'r When thou art nigh.
Come quick - ly and a - bide, Or life is vain.
And thy rich prom - is - es In me ful - fill.

I need thee, oh, I need thee; Ev - 'ry hour I need thee!

Oh, bless me now, my Sav - ior; I come to thee.

Text: Annie S. Hawks and Robert Lowry. Tune and Setting: Robert Lowry.

I Shall Not Be in Want

(Es Yahvé mi Pastor)

fresh me_____ and you lead me in - to
pare for_____ me a ta - ble in the
live with_____ you for - ev - er in your

jus - tice_____ for your name's sake, O Lord!_____
pres - ence_____ of my foes, O my Shep - herd!
dwell - ing,_____ O my God and my Shep - herd.

I shall not be_____ in want; you are my

shep - herd. I shall herd.

Text: tr. Gracia Grindal. Tune: from *Veintiun Cantos Liturgicos 9*.

Es Yahvé mi Pastor
(I Shall Not Be in Want)

1. Es Yahvé mi Pastor, nada me falta;
   me apacienta en verdes prados,
   Me conduce a las aguas de reposo y
   conforta mi alma.
   Él me guía por las sendas de justicia
   por amor de su nombre.

   Refrain
   ¡Es Yahvé mi Pastor; nada me falta!

2. Aunque pase por valle tenebroso
   ningún mal temeré.
   Junto a mí, tu cayado y tu vara: ellos
   son mi consuelo
   Ante mí, tú preparas una mesa frente
   a mis adversarios.

   Refrain

3. Tú perfumas con óleo mi cabeza, y
   desborda mi copa.
   Sí, la dicha y la gracia me acompañan
   por los días de mi vida.
   Viviré en la casa del Señor a través de
   los días.

   Refrain

I Want to Walk as a Child of the Light

1. I want to walk as a child of the light;
2. I want to see the bright-ness of God;
3. I'm look-ing for the com-ing of Christ;

I want to fol - low Je - sus.
I want to look at Je - sus.
I want to be with Je - sus.

God set the stars to give light to the world; The
Clear Sun of Right-eous - ness, shine on my path, And
When we have run with pa - tience the race, We

star of my life is Je - sus.
show me the way to the Fa - ther.
shall know the joy of Je - sus.

142

In him there is no dark-ness at all; The
night and the day— are both a - like. The
Lamb is the light of the cit - y of God.
Shine in my heart, Lord Je - sus.

Text, Tune (HOUSTON), Setting: Kathleen Thomerson.

I Will Call Upon the Lord

saved from my en - e - mies.___ I will call up - on___ the

___ I will call up - on___ the

1.

2.

Lord.

Lord.

The

Lord liv - eth, and bless - ed be the Rock,___ and may the God___

Text, Tune, Setting: Michael O'Shields.
Text, Tune, Setting: © 1981 Sound III. Used by permission of The Lorenz Corp.

I Will Celebrate

Text, Tune, Setting: Linda Duvall.

I Will Sing of the Mercies

I will sing of the mer-cies of the Lord for-ev-er. I will

sing, I will sing, I will sing of the mer-cies of the

Lord for-ev-er. I will sing of the mer-cies of the Lord.___ With my

Tune and Setting: James H. Fillmore.

In My Life, Lord, Be Glorified

1. In my life, Lord, be glo-ri-fied,
2. In my song, Lord, be glo-ri-fied,
3. In your church, Lord, be glo-ri-fied,

be glo-ri-fied. In my life, Lord,
be glo-ri-fied. In my song, Lord,
be glo-ri-fied. In your church, Lord,

1., 2.
3.

be glo-ri-fied to - day.____
be glo-ri-fied to - day.____
be glo-ri-fied to - day.____

4. In my
5. In my

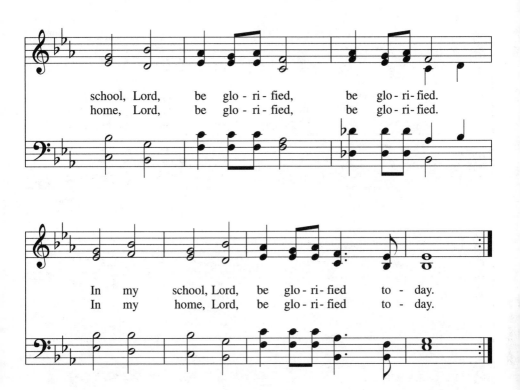

school, Lord, be glo-ri-fied, be glo-ri-fied.
home, Lord, be glo-ri-fied, be glo-ri-fied.

In my school, Lord, be glo-ri-fied to-day.
In my home, Lord, be glo-ri-fied to-day.

Text, Tune, Setting: Bob Kilpatrick.
Text, Tune, Setting: © 1978 Bob Kilpatrick Music. Used by permission of The Lorenz Corp.

Infant Holy, Infant Lowly

1. In - fant ho - ly, in - fant low - ly, for his
2. Flocks were sleep - ing, shep - herds keep - ing vig - il

bed a cat - tle stall; Ox - en low - ing, lit - tle
till the morn - ing new Saw the glo - ry, heard the

know - ing Christ the child is Lord of all. Swift are
sto - ry, tid - ings of a gos - pel true. Thus re -

wing - ing   an - gels   sing - ing,   bells are   ring - ing,   tid - ings
joic - ing,   free from   sor - row,   prais - es   voic - ing,   greet the

bring - ing: Christ   the   child   is   Lord   of
mor - row: Christ   the   child   was   born   for

all,   Christ the   child   is   Lord   of   all.
you,   Christ the   child   was   born   for   you.

Text: traditional Polish carol; tr. Edith M. G. Reed. Tune: traditional Polish carol. Setting: Joseph Barlow.

It Is Well with My Soul

1. When peace, like a riv - er, at - tend - eth my
2. My sin— oh, the joy of this glo - ri - ous
3. And, Lord, haste the day when my faith— shall be

way, When sor - rows like sea bil - lows roll— What -
thought— My sin, not in part, but the whole, Is
sight, The clouds be rolled back as a scroll; The

ev - er my lot, thou hast taught me to
nailed to the cross, and I bear it no
trump shall re - sound and the Lord shall de -

say, It is well, it is well with my soul.
more: Praise the Lord, praise the Lord, O my soul!
scend; E - ven so, it is well with my soul.

It is well_____ with my soul._____

It is well with my

___ It is well, it is well with my soul.

soul.

Text: Horatio G. Spafford. Tune (VILLE DU HAVRE): Philip P. Bliss.

Jesu, Jesu, Fill Us with Your Love

Refrain

Je - su,⎯ Je - su,⎯ fill us with your love, show us how to serve the neigh - bors we have from you.

Verse

1. Kneels at the feet of his friends, si - lent - ly wash - es their feet, mas - ter who acts as a slave⎯ to them.⎯
2. Neigh - bors are rich folk and poor; neigh - bors are black, brown, and white; neigh - bors are near - by and far⎯ a - way.⎯
3. These are the ones we should serve; these are the ones we should love; all these are neigh - bors to us⎯ and you.⎯
4. Lov - ing puts us on our knees, serv - ing as though we are slaves; this is the way we should live⎯ with you.⎯

Text: Tom Colvin. Tune: Ghanaian; adapt. Tom Colvin. Setting: Jane Marshall.

Jesus, Lead Me Day by Day

1. Je - sus, lead me day by day, Ev - er in your own sweet way. Teach me to be pure and true; Show me what I ought to do.

2. When I'm tempt - ed to do wrong, Make me stead - fast, wise, and strong; And when all a - lone I stand, Shield me with your might - y hand.

3. When the day is fresh and new, Help me to re - mem - ber you, Hap - py most of all to know That my Je - sus loves me so.

Tune (POSEN) and Setting: George C. Strattner.

Jesus Loves Me

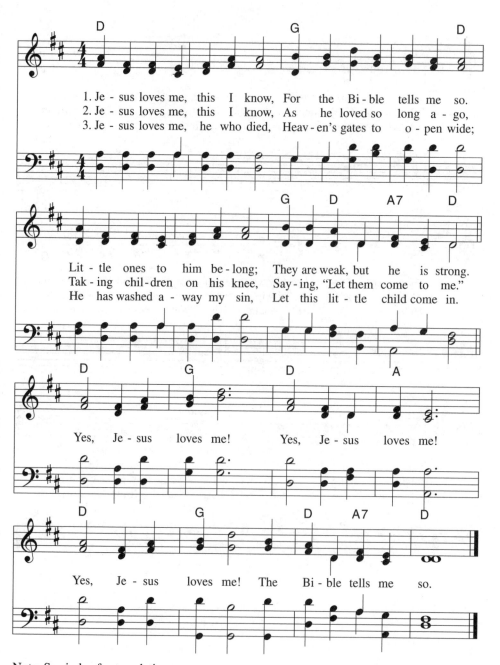

1. Je - sus loves me, this I know, For the Bi - ble tells me so.
2. Je - sus loves me, this I know, As he loved so long a - go,
3. Je - sus loves me, he who died, Heav - en's gates to o - pen wide;

Lit - tle ones to him be - long; They are weak, but he is strong.
Tak - ing chil - dren on his knee, Say - ing, "Let them come to me."
He has washed a - way my sin, Let this lit - tle child come in.

Yes, Je - sus loves me! Yes, Je - sus loves me!

Yes, Je - sus loves me! The Bi - ble tells me so.

Note: See index for translations.

Text: Anna B. Warner, st. 1; David R. McGuire, st. 2,3. Tune and Setting: William B. Bradbury.

Jesus Loves Me, Jesus Loves Me

1. Je - sus loves me, Je - sus loves me; He is al - ways,
2. Je - sus loves me; night and morn - ing Je - sus hears the
3. Je - sus loves me, and he watch - es O - ver me with
4. Je - sus loves me; O Lord Je - sus, Now I pray that

al - ways near. If I do but trust and love him,
prayers I pray, And he nev - er, nev - er leaves me
lov - ing eye, And he sends his ho - ly an - gels
by your love, Keep me ev - er pure and ho - ly,

There is noth - ing___ I need fear.
When I work or___ when I play.
Safe to keep me___ till I die.
Till I come to___ you a - bove.

Tune and Setting: Charlotte A. Barnard.

Jesus Loves the Little Children

1. Je - sus loves the lit - tle chil - dren, All the chil - dren of the world.
2. Je - sus died for lit - tle chil - dren, All the chil - dren of the world.
3. Je - sus rose for lit - tle chil - dren, All the chil - dren of the world.

Red and yel - low, black and white— They are pre - cious in his sight.

Je - sus loves the lit - tle chil - dren of the world.
Je - sus died for lit - tle chil - dren of the world.
Je - sus rose for lit - tle chil - dren of the world.

Tune and Setting: George F. Root.

Jesus, Name above All Names

1. Je - sus, name a - bove all names, Beau - ti - ful Sav - ior, glo - ri - ous Lord,_____ Im - man - u - el, God_____ is with_____ us, Bless - ed Re - deem - er, liv - ing Word.

2. Je - sus, lov - ing Shep - herd, Vine of the branch - es, Son_____ of God,_____ Prince of peace, Won - der - ful Coun - se - lor, Lord of the u - ni - verse, Light of the world.

3. Je - sus, way of sal - va - tion, King_____ of kings,_____ Lord_____ of lords,_____ Way, the Truth, and_____ the Life,_____ Might - y Cre - a - tor, my Sav - ior and friend.

Jesus, Remember Me

Je - sus, re - mem - ber me When you come in - to your king - dom. Je - sus, re - mem - ber me When you come in - to your king - dom.

Tune and Setting: Jacques Berthier.
Text, Tune, Setting: © 1981 Les Presses de Taizé, GIA Publications, agent for the USA. Used by permission.

Jesus, Take Us to the Mountain

1. Je - sus, take us to the moun - tain, Where, with Pe - ter,
2. What do you want us to see there That your close com -
3. What do you want us to hear there That your dear dis -
4. Take us to that oth - er moun - tain Where we see you
5. We who have be - held your glo - ry, Ris - en and as -

James, and John, We are daz - zled by your glo - ry,
pan - ions saw? Your di - vin - i - ty re - vealed there
ci - ples heard? Once a - gain the voice from heav - en
glo - ri - fied, Where you shout - ed, "It is fin - ished!"
cend - ed Lord, Can - not help but tell the sto - ry,

Light as blind - ing as the sun. There pre - pare us
Fills us with the self - same awe. Clothed in flesh like
Says of the in - car - nate Word: "Lis - ten, lis - ten,
Where for all the world you died. Hear the stunned cen -
All that we have seen and heard, Say with Pe - ter,

for the night— By the vi - sion of_____ that sight.
ours you go,— Matched to meet our dead - liest foe.
ev - 'ry - one;— This is my be - lov - ed Son!"
tu - ri - on:— "Tru - ly this was God's____ own Son!"
James, and John:— "You are God's be - lov - ed Son!"

Joyful, Joyful, We Adore Thee

1. Joy - ful, joy - ful, we a - dore thee,
2. All thy works with joy sur - round thee;
3. Thou art giv - ing and for - giv - ing,

God of glo - ry, Lord of love; Hearts un - fold like
Earth and heav'n re - flect thy rays; Stars and an - gels
Ev - er bless - ing, ev - er blest, Well - spring of the

flow'rs be - fore thee, Op'n - ing to the sun a - bove.
sing a - round thee, Cen - ter of un - brok - en praise.
joy of liv - ing, O - cean depth of hap - py rest!

Text: Henry van Dyke. Tune (HYMN TO JOY): Ludwig van Beethoven. Setting: Edward Hodges.

Just a Closer Walk with Thee

1. I am weak, but thou art strong; Je - sus, keep me
2. Through this world of toil and snares, If I fal - ter,
3. When my fee - ble life is o'er, Time for me will
Refrain: Just a clos - er walk with thee, Grant it, Je - sus,

from all wrong;_____ I'll be sat - is - fied as
Lord, who cares?_____ Who with me my bur - den
be no more;_____ Guide me gen - tly, safe - ly
is my plea._____ Dai - ly walk - ing close to

long_____ As I walk, let me walk close to thee.
shares?_____ None but thee, dear___ Lord, none but thee.
o'er_____ To thy king - dom___ shore, to thy shore.
thee, _____ Let it be, dear___ Lord, let it be.

Text, Tune, Setting: traditional.

King of Kings

Note: Sing the song through once in unison. Then, on the repeat, sing as a round.

Text: Naomi Yah and Sophie Conty. Tune: ancient Hebrew folk song.

Lamb of God

1. Your on - ly Son no sin to hide, But you have
2. Your gift of love they cru - ci - fied; They laughed and
3. I was so lost I should have died, But you have

sent him from your side To walk up - on this guilt - y
scorned him as he died; The hum - ble King they named a
brought me to your side To be led by your staff and

sod And to be - come the Lamb of God.
fraud And sac - ri - ficed the Lamb of God.
rod And to be called a lamb of God.

O Lamb of God, sweet Lamb of God, I love the
ho - ly Lamb of God. Oh, wash me in his pre - cious
blood, My Je - sus Christ, the Lamb of God.

Text, Tune, Setting: Twila Paris.

Lead Me, Guide Me

1., 2., 3. Lead— me, guide— me a - long the way,

For— if you lead me, I can - not stray.

Lord,— let me walk each day with thee;

Lead me, O Lord, lead me.

1. I am weak, and I need thy strength and
2. Help me tread in the paths of right - eous -
3. I am lost if you take your hand from

pow'r To help me o - ver my
ness; Be my aid when Sa - tan and
me; I am blind with - out thy

172

weak - est hour. Help me through the
sin op - press. I am put - ting
light to see. Lord, just al - ways

dark - ness thy face to see;
all_____ my trust in thee;
let me thy ser - vant be;

Lead me, O Lord,___ lead me.___
Lead me, O Lord,___ lead me.___
Lead me, O Lord,___ lead me.___

Text, Tune, Setting: Doris M. Akers.

Leaning on the Everlasting Arms

1. What a fel-low-ship, what a joy di-vine,
2. Oh, how sweet to walk in this pil-grim way,
3. What have I to dread, what have I to fear,

Lean - ing on the ev - er - last - ing arms;
Lean - ing on the ev - er - last - ing arms;
Lean - ing on the ev - er - last - ing arms?

What a bless - ed-ness, what a peace is mine,
Oh, how bright the path grows from day to day,
I have bless - ed peace with my Lord so near,

Lean - ing on the ev - er - last - ing arms.
Lean - ing on the ev - er - last - ing arms.
Lean - ing on the ev - er - last - ing arms.

174

Leaning, leaning, safe and secure from

Lean-ing on Je-sus, lean-ing on Je-sus,

all a-larms; Lean - ing, lean - ing,

Lean - ing on Je - sus, lean-ing on Je - sus,

lean - ing on the ev - er - last - ing arms.

Text: Elisha A. Hoffman. Tune (SHOWALTER) and Setting: Anthony J. Showalter.

Let Me Learn of Jesus

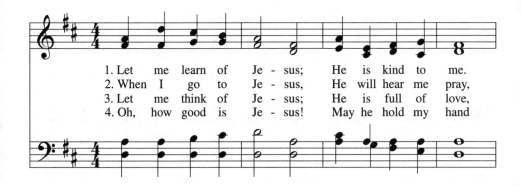

1. Let me learn of Je - sus; He is kind to me.
2. When I go to Je - sus, He will hear me pray,
3. Let me think of Je - sus; He is full of love,
4. Oh, how good is Je - sus! May he hold my hand

Once he died to save me, Nailed up - on the tree.
Make me pure and ho - ly, Take my sins a - way.
Look - ing down up - on me From his throne a - bove.
And at last re - ceive me To a bet - ter land.

Text: Fanny J. Crosby. Tune and Setting: James F. Swift.

Let the Peace of Christ Rule in Your Heart

Let the peace of Christ rule in your heart, Let the peace of Christ rule in your heart,—— And what-ev-er you do in—— word or—— deed, Do it all in the name of the Lord,—— Giv-ing thanks, giv-ing thanks—— to God through—— Christ the——

Lord,_____ Giv - ing thanks, giv - ing thanks to God through___ Christ the___ Lord.

Text, Tune, Setting: Benny Cagle.

Let There Be Light

1. Let there be light; Let all the na - tions gath - er; Let there be un - der - stand - ing;
2. O - pen our lips; O - pen our minds to pon - der; O - pen the door of con - cord
3. Per - ish the sword; Per - ish the an - gry judg - ment; Per - ish the bombs and hun - ger;
4. Let there be light; O - pen our hearts to won - der; Per - ish the way of ter - ror;

Let them be face - to -
O - pen - ing in - to
Per - ish the fight for
Hal - low the world God

face.
grace.
gain.
made.

last time

last time

Let There Be Praise

love, it knows no end. So lift your voic - es;
praise is on our tongue. So lift your voic - es;

with glad - ness sing. Pro - claim through
with glad - ness sing. Pro - claim through

all the earth___ that Je - sus Christ is King!
all the earth___ that Je - sus Christ is King!

Text, Tune, Setting: Dick Tunney and Melodie Tunney.

Let Us Break Bread Together

1. Let us break bread to-geth-er on our knees,
2. Let us drink wine to-geth-er on our knees,
3. Let us praise God to-geth-er on our knees,

Let us break bread to-geth-er on our knees.
Let us drink wine to-geth-er on our knees.
Let us praise God to-geth-er on our knees.

When I fall on my knees with my face to the ris-ing

sun, O Lord, have mer-cy on me.

Text and Tune: African-American spiritual.
Setting: from *Contemporary Worship 4: Hymns for Baptism and Holy Communion* © 1972 Augsburg Fortress. Used by permission.

Let Your Heart Be Broken

1. Let your heart be bro - ken For a world in
2. Here on earth ap - ply - ing Prin - ci - ples of
3. Blest to be a bless - ing, Priv - i - leged to
4. Add to your be - liev - ing Deeds that prove it
5. Let your heart be ten - der And your vi - sion

need— Feed the mouths that hun - ger,
love— Vis - i - ble ex - pres - sion
care, Chal - lenged by the need Ap -
true— Know - ing Christ as Sav - ior,
clear— See man - kind as God sees;

Soothe the wounds that bleed, Give the cup of
God still rules a - bove, Liv - ing il - lus -
par - ent ev - 'ry - where— Where man - kind is
Make him mas - ter too: Fol - low in his
Serve him far and near. Let your heart be

wa - ter And the— loaf of bread. Be the— hands of
tra - tion Of the— liv - ing Word To the— minds of
want - ing, Fill the— va - cant place; Be the— means through
foot - steps; Go where— he has trod; In the— world's great
bro - ken By a— broth - er's pain; Share your— rich re -

Je - sus, Serv - ing— in his stead.
all who've Nev - er— seen and heard.
which the Lord re - veals his grace.
trou - ble, Risk your - self for God.
sourc - es— Give and— give a - gain.

Text: Bryan Jeffery Leech. Tune (CRYSTAL) and Setting: John Vanderhoven.
Text: © 1975 The Evangelical Covenant Church. Used by permission.

Lift Every Voice and Sing

Sing a song full of the faith that the dark past has taught us;
Lest our feet stray from the plac-es, our God, where we met thee,

Sing a song full of the hope that the pres-ent has brought us.
Lest our hearts, drunk with the wine of the world, we for-get thee.

Fac-ing the ris-ing sun of our new day be-gun,
Shad-owed be-neath thy hand, may we for-ev-er stand

Let us march on till vic-to-ry is won.
True to our God, true to our na - tive land.

Text: James Weldon Johnson. Tune and Setting: J. Rosamond Johnson.

Listen to My Prayer, O Lord

1. Lis - ten to my prayer, O Lord,_____ and hear my sigh.
2. Lord, please let me do your will;_____ make your way plain.

Lis - ten to my prayer, O Lord,_____ and hear my voice._____

Save me from my en - e - mies,_____ and hear my voice._____ Be - cause of

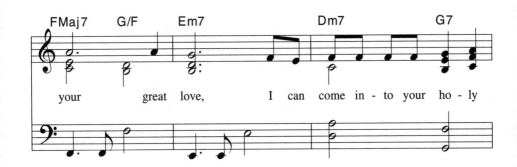

your great love, I can come in - to your ho - ly

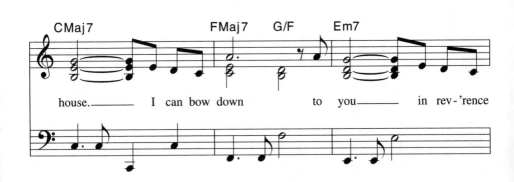

house.———— I can bow down to you———— in rev-'rence

meant for you. Lis-ten to my prayer.————

Tune and Setting: Handt Hanson.

The Lord Is My Light

1. The Lord is my light___ and my sal - va - tion—
2. I ask of the Lord___ for on - ly one thing,
3. Come hear me, O Lord,___ when - e'er I call you;

whom shall I fear? The Lord is the strong - hold of my life.
this will I seek: to live in the Lord's___ house all my life.
an - swer me, Lord. I come to you now;___ I seek your face.

For he will hide___ me, and he will guide___ me;
In times of trou - ble he will pro - tect___ me;
Since you have helped___ me in all my tri - als,

he will set me high___ up - on a rock. The
he will keep me safe___ from ev - 'ry foe. I
do not leave me now,___ O Lord, my life. Come

Lord is my light___ and my sal - va - tion—
ask of the Lord___ for on - ly one thing,
hear me, O Lord,___ when - e'er I call you;

whom shall I fear? The Lord is the strong -
this will I seek: to live in the Lord's___
an - swer me, Lord. I come to you now;—

hold of my life.
house all my life.
I seek your face.

Text: Marjorie Jillson. Tune and Setting: Heinz Werner Zimmermann.
Text, Tune, Setting: from *Five Psalm Settings* © 1973 Concordia Publishing House. Used by permission.

The Lord Is Present in His Sanctuary

1. The Lord is pres-ent in his sanc - tu - ar - y;
2. The Lord is pres-ent in his sanc - tu - ar - y;
3. The Lord is pres-ent in his sanc - tu - ar - y;

Let us praise_____ the Lord. The Lord is pres - ent in his
Let us de-light in the Lord. The Lord is pres - ent in his
Let us serve_____ the Lord. The Lord is pres - ent in his

sanc - tu - ar - y; Let us praise_____ the Lord.
sanc - tu - ar - y; Let us de-light in the Lord.
sanc - tu - ar - y; Let us serve_____ the Lord.

Praise him, praise—— him.—— Let us praise—— the Lord.——

Praise him, praise—— him.—— Let us praise—— Je - sus.

Text, Tune, Setting: Gail Cole.

Love Is His Word

1. Love is his word; love is his way.
2. Love is his way; love is his mark.
3. Love is his mark; love is his sign.
4. Love is his sign; love is his news.
5. Love is his news; love is his name.
6. Love is his name; love is his law.
7. Love is his law; love is his word:

Feast - ing with all, fast - ing a - lone,
Shar - ing his last Pass - o - ver feast,
Bread for our strength, wine for our joy.
"Do this," he said, "lest you for - get
We are his own, cho - sen and called,
Hear his com - mand, all who are his:
Love of the Lord, Fa - ther and Word,

Liv - ing and dy - ing, ris - ing a - gain.
Guest at his ta - ble, host to the Twelve.
"This is my bod - y; this is my blood."
All my deep sor - row, all my dear blood."
Fam - i - ly, breth - ren, cous - ins, and kin.
"Love one an - oth - er; I have loved you."
Love of the Spir - it, God Three in One.

Love, on - ly love, is his way.
Love, on - ly love, is his mark.
Love, on - ly love, is his sign.
Love, on - ly love, is his news.
Love, on - ly love, is his name.
Love, on - ly love, is his law.
Love, on - ly love, is his word.

Rich - er than gold is the love of my Lord,

Bet - ter than splen-dor and wealth. Rich - er than gold is the

love of my Lord, Bet - ter than splen-dor and wealth.

Text: Luke Connaughton. Tune and Setting: Robert M. Hutmacher.

Lovely Child, Holy Child

Al - le - lu - ia, al - le - lu - ia,

Al - le - lu - ia, al - le - lu - ia!

Low in the Grave He Lay

1. Low in the grave he lay, Je - sus, my Sav - ior!
2. Vain - ly they watched his bed, Je - sus, my Sav - ior!
3. Death could not keep his prey, Je - sus, my Sav - ior!

Wait - ing the com - ing day, Je - sus, my Lord!
Vain - ly they sealed the dead, Je - sus, my Lord!
He tore the bars a - way, Je - sus, my Lord!

Up from the grave he a - rose, With a

he a - rose!

might - y tri - umph o'er his foes, He a -

he a - rose!

rose a vic - tor from the dark do - main, And he

lives for - ev - er with his saints to reign. He a -

rose! He a - rose!   Hal - le -

He a - rose!   He a - rose!

lu - jah! Christ a - rose!

Text: Robert Lowry. Tune (CHRIST AROSE) and Setting: Robert Lowry.

Majesty

So ex - alt, lift up on high the name of Je - sus.

Mag - ni - fy, come glo - ri - fy Christ Je - sus the King.

Maj - es - ty, wor - ship his maj - es - ty,

Je - sus, who died, now glo - ri - fied, King of all kings.

Text and Tune: Jack Hayford. Setting: Eugene Thomas.

Make Me a Servant

Make me a ser-vant, hum-ble and meek;

Lord, let me lift up those who are__ weak.

And may the prayer of my heart al-ways be:

Make me a ser-vant, make me a ser-vant,

Make me a ser-vant to - day.__

Text, Tune, Setting: Kelly Willard.

Man of Sorrows, What a Name

1. "Man of Sor-rows," what a name For the Son of God, who came Ru-ined sin-ners to re-claim! Hal-le-lu-jah! What a Sav-ior!
2. Bear-ing shame and scoff-ing rude, In my place con-demned he stood, Sealed my par-don with his blood. Hal-le-lu-jah! What a Sav-ior!
3. Guilt-y, vile, and help-less, we; Spot-less Lamb of God was he. "Full a-tone-ment," can it be? Hal-le-lu-jah! What a Sav-ior!
4. Lift-ed up was he to die; "It is fin-ished" was his cry; Now in heav'n ex-alt-ed high. Hal-le-lu-jah! What a Sav-ior!
5. When he comes, our glo-rious King, All his ran-somed home to bring, Then a-new this song we'll sing: Hal-le-lu-jah! What a Sav-ior!

Text, Tune, Setting: Philip P. Bliss.

Mary's Little Boy Child

1. Long time a - go____ in____ Beth - le - hem,__ So the
(2.) Shep - herds__ watched__ their__ flocks by night, __ Heav-en
(3.) Jo - seph__ and__ his__ wife, Mar - y, __ Came to
4. By and__ by they found a lit - tle nook__ In a

Ho - ly Bi - ble say, Mar - y's boy child,
o - pened up with love. They heard a choir from
Beth - le - hem that night. They found no place to
sta - ble all for - lorn, And in a man - ger,

Je - sus Christ,- Was born on Christ - mas Day.
heav-en sing;__ The mu - sic came from a - bove.
bear her child;__ Not a sin - gle room was in sight.
cold and dark,__ Mar - y's lit - tle boy child was born.

205

1. Hark! Now hear the an-gels sing. New King is born to-day.—
2. Hark! Now hear the an-gels sing. New King is born to-day.—
4. Trum-pets sound and an-gels sing. Lis - ten to what they say,—

— And we will live for - ev - er-more— Be -
— And we will live for - ev - er-more— Be -
— That we will live for - ev - er-more— Be -

cause of Christ - mas Day. 2. While
cause of Christ - mas Day. 3. Now
cause of Christ - mas Day.

Text, Tune, Setting: Jester Hairston.

The Moon with Borrowed Light

1. The moon with bor - rowed light Gives wit - ness to the sun, Dis - creet - ly fad - ing with the night When morn - ing has be - gun.

2. The tem - ple Le - vites asked What ti - tle did John claim. He said he had a sin - gle task, A sin - gle goal and aim:

3. The clouds of sin yet mask Earth's tan - gled, stub - bly ground, And, oh, how man - y hearts still ask Where God's clear path is found.

John's bor-rowed light was drawn From heav-en's vi-brant rays,—
To re-di-rect their sight Be-yond what he had done—
For bor-rowed light we pray, So we may be a sign—

His life a wit-ness to the
To Christ the pure and pri-mal
That points to Christ, the truth, the

dawn Of Christ's ap-proach-ing blaze.
light That light - ens ev - 'ry - one.
way, The life, the light di - vine.

Text: Thomas H. Troeger. Tune and Setting: Carol Doran.
Text, Tune, Setting: from *New Songs for the Lectionary* © 1985 Oxford University Press. Used by permission.

My Lord, What a Morning

Refrain

My Lord, what a morn-ing! My Lord, what a morn-ing!—

My Lord, what a morn-ing, When the stars be-gin— to fall.

Verse

1. You'll— hear the trum-pet— sound— To wake the
2. You'll— hear the sin-ner— cry— To wake the
3. You'll— hear the an-gel— shout— To wake the

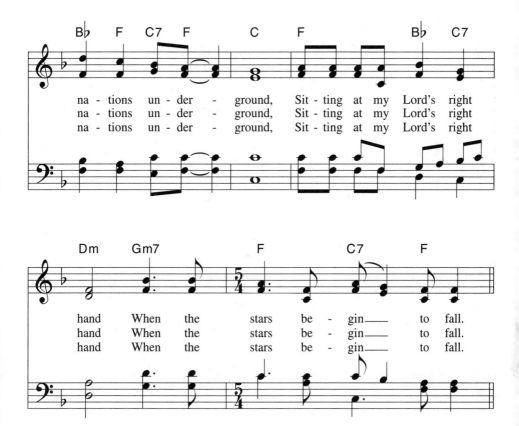

na - tions un - der - ground, Sit - ting at my Lord's right
na - tions un - der - ground, Sit - ting at my Lord's right
na - tions un - der - ground, Sit - ting at my Lord's right

hand When the stars be - gin___ to fall.
hand When the stars be - gin___ to fall.
hand When the stars be - gin___ to fall.

Text and Tune: African-American spiritual.

No Mountain High Enough

There is no moun-tain high e-nough,— No riv-er

wide e-nough,— No o-cean deep e-nough— To

sep - a - rate me from God. There is God.

1. No des - ert dry e-nough, No jun - gle thick e-nough,
2. No king is great e-nough, No ar - my large e-nough,

No e-vil bad e-nough To keep me from my Lord.
No pow-er strong e-nough To keep me from my Lord. There is

no moun-tain high e-nough,— No riv-er wide e-nough,—

No o-cean deep e-nough— To sep-a-rate me from

God. God, To sep-a-rate me from God.

Jesus Loves Me
(Tonga translation)

1. Jesu ulandiyanda,
   Lila'mba ibaibele,
   Twana toonse ntutwakwe,
   Ulatupa inguzu.

   Refrain
   Ulandiyanda
   Ndayandwa Jesu
   Ulandiyanda
   Lila'mba ibaibele.

2. Jesu ulandiyanda,
   Jesu wakandifwida;
   Ulakunditubya bu;
   Atunjile twanakwe.

   Refrain

3. Jesu ulandiyanda,
   No ndaciswa bunene;
   Mu cuuno ca kujulu
   Ulaboola kuli 'me.

   Refrain

4. Jesu ulandiyanda,
   Ulandisololela;
   Kuti ndamuyandisya,
   Ndilakutolwa kwakwe.

   Refrain

Pronunciation guide:
a = *a* as in *father*
e = *a* as in *gate*
i = *i* as in *machine*
o = *o* as in *low*
u = *oo* as in *zoo*

Tonga translation from *Nyiimbo zya Bantu Botatwe*, Lutheran Press, Lutheran Church of Central Africa. Used by permission.

Now Let the Heavens Be Joyful

1. Now let the heav'ns be joy - ful, Let____ earth its song be - gin, The round world keep high tri - umph, And____ all that is there - in.

2. From death to life e - ter - nal, From____ earth on to the sky, Our Christ has brought us o - ver With____ hymns of vic - to - ry. He is ris - en! He is ris - en!

3. Let all things seen and un - seen Their____ notes of glad - ness blend, For Christ the Lord is ris - en; Our____ joy shall have no end.

Christ the____ Lord is ris - en! Our joy shall have no end.

Text: John of Damascus; tr. John Mason Neale, alt. Tune: Provençal carol. Setting: Healey Willan.

Oh, Give Us Homes

1. Oh, give us homes built firm - ly on the Sav - ior,
2. Oh, give us homes where Christ is Lord and mas - ter,
3. O Lord, our God, our homes are yours for - ev - er!

Where Christ is head and coun - sel - or and guide,
The Bi - ble read, the pre - cious hymns still sung,
We trust to you their prob - lems, toil, and care;

Where ev - 'ry child is taught his love and fa - vor
Where prayer comes first in peace or in dis - as - ter
Their bonds of love no en - e - my can sev - er

And gives his heart to Christ, the cru - ci - fied.
And praise is nat - ural speech to ev - 'ry tongue,
If you are al - ways Lord and mas - ter there.

How sweet to know that, though our foot-steps wa - ver,
Where moun - tains move be - fore a faith that's vast - er
Lord, be the cen - ter of our least en - deav - or;

A faith - ful Lord is walk - ing by our side!
And Christ suf - fi - cient is for old and young.
Lord, be our guest, our hearts and homes to share.

Text: Barbara B. Hart. Tune (FINLANDIA): Jean Sibelius.

Text: © 1985 Singspiration Music. All rights reserved. Used by permission of Brentwood-Benson Music Publishing. Tune: © Breitkopf & Härtel, Wiesbaden-Leipzig. Used by permission. Setting: from *The Hymnbook* © 1933, 1961 Presbyterian Board of Christian Education. Used by permission of Westminster/John Knox Press.

Oh, He's King of Kings

Refrain

Oh, he's King of kings! Oh, he's Lord of lords!
Je - sus Christ, the first and last,— No man works like him.

Verse

1. I know that my Re - deem - er lives,— No man works like him, And
2. Vic - to - ri - ous at God's right hand,— No man works like him, He
3. Re - pent, O sin - ner, and be - lieve,— No man works like him; Grace

by his love sweet bless - ings gives,— No man works like him.
calls his saints from ev - 'ry land,— No man works like him.
of the Lord you will re - ceive,— No man works like him.

Text and Tune: African-American spiritual.

Oh, How Good Is Christ the Lord
(Oh, qué bueno es Jesús)

Oh, how good— is Christ the Lord! On the cross— he died for me.
¡Oh, qué bue - no es Je - sús! Que por mí mu - rió en la cruz.

He has par - doned all my sin. Glo - ry be— to Je - sus!
Mis pe - ca - dos per - do - nó. ¡A su nom - bre glo - ria!

Glo - ry be— to Je - sus! Glo - ry be— to Je - sus!
¡A su nom - bre glo - ria! ¡A su nom - bre glo - ria!

In three days— he rose a - gain. Glo - ry be— to Je - sus!
En tres días— re - su - ci - tó. ¡A su nom - bre glo - ria!

Text and Tune: Puerto Rican folk hymn. Setting: Dale Grotenhuis.
Setting: © 1987 CRC Publications. Used by permission.

Oh, How He Loves You and Me

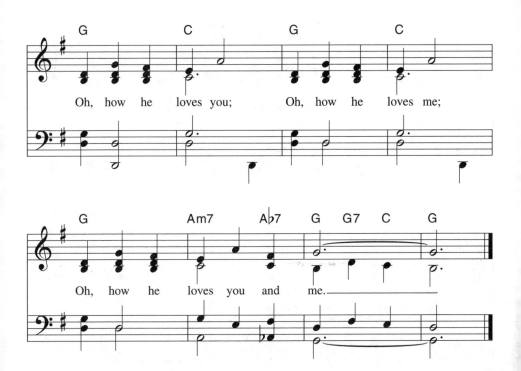

Oh, How I Love Jesus

1. There is a name I love to hear; I love to sing its worth. It sounds like music in my ear, The sweet - est name on earth.

2. It tells me of a Sav - ior's love, Who died to set me free; It tells me of his pre - cious blood, The sin - ner's per - fect plea.

3. It tells of one whose lov - ing heart Can feel my deep - est woe, Who in each sor - row bears a part That none can bear be - low.

Oh, how I love Je - sus. Oh, how I love

Je - sus.———— Oh, how I love Je - sus— Be -

cause———— he first loved me!————

Text: Frederick Whitfield. Tune: American melody.

Oh, Magnify the Lord

1. Oh, mag - ni - fy,___ Oh, mag - ni - fy___ the Lord___ with
2. Oh, wor - ship him,___ Oh, wor - ship Christ___ the Lord___ with

me, And let us ex - alt his name to - geth - er!
me, And let us ex - alt his name to - geth - er!

Oh, mag - ni - fy___ the Lord, Oh, mag - ni - fy___ the
Oh, wor - ship Christ___ the Lord; Oh, wor - ship Christ___ the

last time to Coda

Lord, And may his name be lift - ed___ high for - ev -
Lord; And may his name be lift - ed___ high for - ev -

er! er! King of kings and Lord— of— lords, May his name be lift-ed— high for-

D.C. al Coda

ev - er!

Coda

ev - er!___

Oh, Sing to the Lord

(Cantad al Señor)

1. Oh, sing to the Lord; Oh, sing God a new song. Oh, sing to the Lord; Oh, sing God a new song. Oh, sing to the Lord; Oh, sing God a
2. For God is the Lord, And he has done won-ders. For God is the Lord, And he has done won-ders. For God is the Lord, And he has done
3. So dance for our God And blow all the trum-pets. So dance for our God And blow all the trum-pets. So dance for our God And blow all the
4. Oh, shout to our God, Who gave us the Spir-it. Oh, shout to our God, Who gave us the Spir-it. Oh, shout to our God, Who gave us the
5. For Je-sus is Lord! A - men! Al - le - lu - ia! For Je-sus is Lord! A - men! Al - le - lu - ia! For Je-sus is Lord! A - men! Al - le -

	Am			Em	B7	Em

new   song. Oh,   sing   to   our   God.   Oh,   sing   to   our   God.
won - ders. Oh,   sing   to   our   God.   Oh,   sing   to   our   God.
trum - pets. And   sing   to   our   God.   And   sing   to   our   God.
Spir - it. Oh,   sing   to   our   God.   Oh,   sing   to   our   God.
lu - ia! Oh,   sing   to   our   God.   Oh,   sing   to   our   God.

1. Cantad al Señor un cántico nuevo,
   Cantad al Señor un cántico nuevo,
   Cantad al Señor un cántico nuevo,
   ¡Cantad al Señor, cantad al Señor!

2. Porque el Señor ha hecho prodigios,
   Porque el Señor ha hecho prodigios,
   Porque el Señor ha hecho prodigios,
   ¡Cantad al Señor, cantad al Señor!

3. Cantad al Señor, alabadle con arpa,
   Cantad al Señor, alabadle con arpa,
   Cantad al Señor, alabadle con arpa,
   ¡Cantad al Señor, cantad al Señor!

4. Es él que nos da el Espíritu Santo,
   Es él que nos da el Espíritu Santo,
   Es él que nos da el Espíritu Santo,
   ¡Cantad al Señor, cantad al Señor!

5. ¡Jesus es Señor! ¡Amen, aleluya!
   ¡Jesus es Señor! ¡Amen, aleluya!
   ¡Jesus es Señor! ¡Amen, aleluya!
   ¡Cantad al Señor, cantad al Señor!

Text: Brazilian folk song; tr. Gerhard Cartford. Tune: Brazilian folk song. Setting: Gerhard Cartford.
Text: tr. © Gerhard Cartford. Used by permission. Setting: from *All God's People Sing* © 1991 Concordia Publishing House. Used by permission.

The Old Rugged Cross

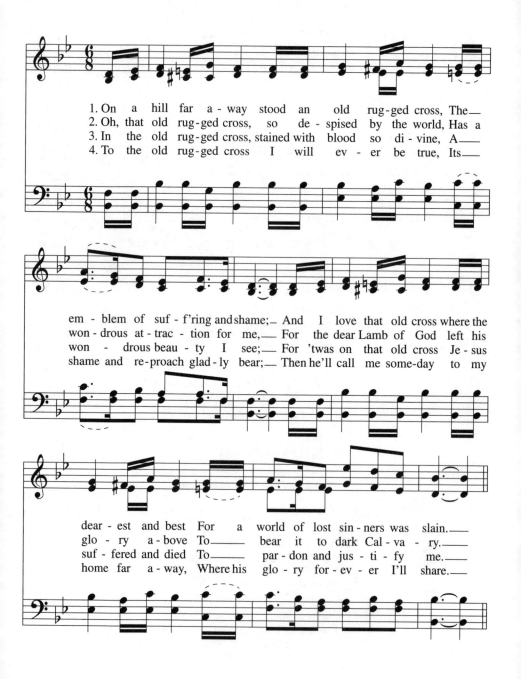

1. On a hill far a - way stood an old rug-ged cross, The—
2. Oh, that old rug-ged cross, so de - spised by the world, Has a
3. In the old rug-ged cross, stained with blood so di - vine, A—
4. To the old rug-ged cross I will ev - er be true, Its—

em - blem of suf - f'ring and shame;— And I love that old cross where the
won - drous at - trac - tion for me,— For the dear Lamb of God left his
won - drous beau - ty I see;— For 'twas on that old cross Je - sus
shame and re-proach glad - ly bear;— Then he'll call me some-day to my

dear - est and best For a world of lost sin - ners was slain.—
glo - ry a - bove To— bear it to dark Cal - va - ry.—
suf - fered and died To— par - don and jus - ti - fy me.—
home far a - way, Where his glo - ry for - ev - er I'll share.—

So I'll cher-ish the old rug-ged cross— Till my tro-phies at last I lay down;— I will cling to the old rug-ged cross— And ex-change it some-day for a crown.—

On This Day Earth Shall Ring

1. On this day earth shall ring
2. His the doom, ours the mirth;
3. God's bright star o'er his head,
4. On this day an - gels sing;

With the song chil - dren sing To the Lord, Christ our King,
When he came down to earth, Beth - le - hem saw his birth;
Wise men there to him led; Kneel-ing low by his bed,
With their song earth shall ring, Prais - ing Christ, heav-en's King,

Born on earth to save us; Him the Fa - ther gave us.
Ox - en close be - side him From the cold would hide him.
Lay their gifts be - fore him, Praise him and a - dore him.
Born on earth to save us. Peace and love he gave us.

Id - e - o,⎯⎯⎯⎯⎯⎯ Id - e - o,⎯⎯⎯⎯⎯

Id - e - o glo - ri - a in ex - cel - sis De - o!

Text: from *Piae Cantiones;* tr. Jane M. Joseph. Tune: from *Piae Cantiones.* Setting: Gustav T. Holst.

Jesus Loves Me
(Japanese translation)

1. Shu ware wo aisu,
   Shu wa tsuyokereba,
   Ware yowakutomo,
   Osore wa araji.

   Refrain
   Waga Shu Yesu,
   Waga Shu Yesu,
   Waga Shu Yesu,
   Ware wo aisu.

2. Waga tsumi no tame,
   Sakae wo sutete,
   Ame yori kudari,
   Jujika ni tsukeri

   Refrain

3. Mikuni no kado wo,
   Hirakite ware wo,
   Maneki-tamaeri,
   Isamite noboran.

   Refrain

4. Waga Kimi Yesu yo,
   Ware wo kiyomete,
   Yoki hataraki wo,
   Nasashime-tamae.

   Refrain

Pronunciation guide:
a = *a* as in *father*
e = *e* as in *bed*
i = *ee* as in *keep*
o = *o* as in *low*
u = *oo* as in *zoo*

Translation by John Kohji Suguiyama. Used by permission.

Once on a Mountaintop

1. Once on a moun-tain-top There stood three star-tled men
2. Yet we have lived and died And found of God no trace.
3. And minds that learn to scan Cre - a - tion like a book

Who saw the veil of na - ture drop And heav'n shine in.
"You are a God," the proph - et cried, "Who hides his face."
Say noth-ing lives out - side their plan, So nev - er look.

Their friend of ev - 'ry day, The— face— they— knew for his,
The earth lies all ex - plored; The— heav-ens are— ours to climb.
O Lord of hid-den light, For - give— us— who des - pise

They saw for just a while the— way He— al - ways is.
And still no one has seen our— God At— an - y time.
The things which lie be - yond our— sight, And— give us eyes.

One Small Child

One small cit - y of life.
One King bring - ing us
One small light from a
One small Sav - ior of life.

1., 4. life.
2., 3. face.

2. See him ly - ing, a
3. See the shep - herds

cra - dle be - neath him. See him smil - ing in— the stall. See his moth - er
kneel - ing be - fore him. See the kings on bend - ed knee. See his moth - er

D.C.

prais - ing his Fa - ther. See his ti - ny eye - lids fall.—
prais - ing his Fa - ther. See the bless - ed in - fant sleep.—

Text, Tune, Setting: David Meece.
Text, Tune, Setting: © 1971 Word Music. All rights reserved. Used by permission.

Our Father in Heaven

1. Our Fa - ther in heav - en, we hal - low your name.
2. For - give our trans - gres - sions and teach us to know

May your king - dom ho - ly on earth be the same.
That hum - ble com - pas - sion which par - dons each foe.

Oh, give to us dai - ly our por - tion of bread.
Keep us from temp - ta - tion, from e - vil and sin,

It is from your boun - ty that all must be fed.
For yours is the glo - ry for - ev - er! A - men.

Text: Sarah J. Hale. Tune (ST. DENIO): from John Robert's *Caniadau y Cyssegr.*

Our Thanks, O God, for Parents

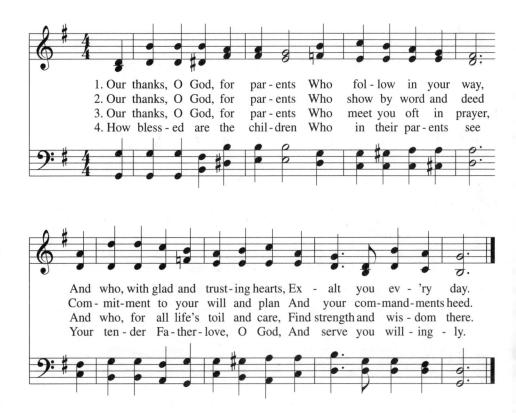

1. Our thanks, O God, for par-ents Who fol-low in your way,
2. Our thanks, O God, for par-ents Who show by word and deed
3. Our thanks, O God, for par-ents Who meet you oft in prayer,
4. How bless-ed are the chil-dren Who in their par-ents see

And who, with glad and trust-ing hearts, Ex - alt you ev - 'ry day.
Com - mit-ment to your will and plan And your com-mand-ments heed.
And who, for all life's toil and care, Find strength and wis - dom there.
Your ten - der Fa-ther-love, O God, And serve you will - ing - ly.

Text, Tune, Setting: Lois S. Johnson.

Pass It On

1. It___ on - ly takes a spark to get a fire___
2. What a won - drous time is spring, when all the trees are
3. I___ wish for you, my friend, this hap - pi - ness that

go - ing,_____ And soon all those a -
bud - ding,_____ The birds be - gin to
I've___ found._____ You can de - pend on

round can warm up in its glow - ing.
sing, the flow - ers start their bloom - ing._____
him; it mat - ters not where you're___ bound._____

That's how it is with God's___ love
That's how it is with God's___ love
I'll shout it from the moun-tain - top!

once you've ex - pe - ri-enced it:___ You spread his love to
once you've ex - pe - ri-enced it:___ You want to sing; it's
I want my world___ to know:___ The Lord of love has

ev - 'ry-one; you want to pass it on.___
fresh like spring; you want to pass it on.___
come to me; I want to pass it on.___

Peace like a River

1. There's a riv-er that brings joy___ To the
2. God's our shel-ter and our strength___ And our
3. Come and see what God has done,___ What a-
4. Glo-ry be to God a-bove,___ Glo-ry

Refrain: I've got peace___ like a riv-er! I've got

cit-y of our God,___ To the sac-ra-men-tal
help in time of trou-ble; Though the earth is shak-en
maz-ing things are done;___ Stop your fight-ing now and
to the God of love,___ Glo-ry be to God the

peace___ like a riv-er! I've got peace___ like a

house of the Most High.___ In that
we will nev-er fear,___ Though the
know that God is Lord!___ Wars are
Spir-it, Three in One!___ As it

riv-er in my soul!___ I've got

cit - y God a - bides;___ It will nev - er be de-
moun - tains tum - ble down___ And the o - ceans roar and
stopped a - round the world,___ Spears de - stroyed and bows are
was when time be - gan,___ It is now and ev - er

peace___ like a riv - er! I've got peace___ like a

stroyed.__ In the morn - ing you will sure - ly draw___ nigh.
rage___ And the hills are shak - en by the noise they hear.
bro - ken; God's su - preme a - mong the na - tions of the world.
shall be; There's a king - dom with - out end.___ A - men!

riv - er! I've got peace___ like a riv - er in my soul!

Text: traditional American; para. John Ylvisaker. Tune: traditional American. Setting: John Ylvisaker.
Text and Setting: from *Songs for Saints* © 1976 Concordia Publishing House. Used by permission.

Praise the Lord Who Reigns Above

1. Praise the Lord who reigns a - bove— And keeps his court be -
2. Cel - e - brate the e - ter - nal God— With harp and psal - ter -
3. Him, in whom they move and live,— Let ev - 'ry crea - ture

low; Praise the ho - ly God of love,— And
y; Tim - brels soft and cym - bals loud— In
sing; Glo - ry to their Mak - er give— And

all his great - ness show; Praise him for his
his high praise a - gree. Praise him ev - 'ry
hom - age to their King. Hal - lowed be his

no - ble—deeds; Praise him— for his match - less—pow'r.
tune - ful—string, All the— reach of heav'n - ly— art;
name be - neath, As in—heav'n on earth— a - dored.

Him from whom all good pro-ceeds— Let earth and—heav'n a - dore.
All the pow'rs of mu - sic bring,— The mu - sic— of the heart.
Praise the Lord in ev - 'ry breath;— Let all things— praise the Lord.

Text: Charles Wesley. Tune (AMSTERDAM): from *Foundery Collection*.

Praise the Lord with the Sound of Trumpet

1. Praise the Lord with the sound of trum-pet; Praise the Lord with the
2. Praise the Lord with the crash-ing cym-bal; Praise the Lord with the

harp and lute; Praise the Lord with the gen-tle-sound-ing
pipe and string; Praise the Lord with the joy-ful songs— you

flute. Praise the Lord in the field and for-est;
sing. Praise the Lord on a week-day morn-ing;

Praise the Lord in the cit-y square; Praise the Lord an-y-
Praise the Lord on a Sun-day noon; Praise the Lord by the

244

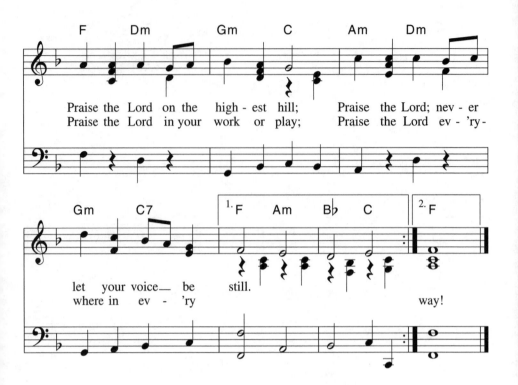

Praise the Lord on the high - est hill;   Praise the Lord; nev - er
Praise the Lord in your work or play;   Praise the Lord ev - 'ry-

let your voice— be still.
where in ev - 'ry way!

People Need the Lord

1. Peo - ple need the Lord; Peo - ple need the
2. Peo - ple need the Lord; Peo - ple need the

Lord. At the end of bro - ken dreams
Lord. When— will we re - al - ize

He's the o - pen door. Peo - ple need the Lord?

Text and Tune: Phill McHugh and Greg Nelson. Setting: David Allen.

Text, Tune, Setting: © 1983 River Oaks Music Co./BMI and Shepherd's Fold Music/BMI. Used by permission of EMI.

Praise the Spirit in Creation

1. Praise the Spir - it in cre - a - tion, Breath of
2. Praise the Spir - it, close com - pan - ion Of our
3. Tell of how the as - cend - ed Je - sus Armed a
4. Pray we then, O Lord the Spir - it, On our

God, life's or - i - gin, Spir - it mov - ing on the
in - most thoughts and ways, Who in show - ing us God's
peo - ple for his own, How a hun - dred men and
lives de - scend in might; Let your flame break out with -

wa - ters, Quick-'ning worlds to life with - in, Source of
won - ders Is him - self the pow'r to gaze, And God's
wom - en Turned the known world up - side down, To its
in us; Fire our hearts and clear our sight Till, white -

breath to all things breath - ing, Life in whom all lives be -
will to those who lis - ten By a still small voice con -
dark and fur - thest cor - ners By the wind of heav - en
hot in your pos - ses - sion, We too set the world a -

gin.
veys.
blown.
light.

Text: Michael Hewlett. Tune (JULION) and Setting: David Hurd.
Text: from *English Praise, 1975.* Used by permission of Oxford University Press. Tune and Setting: © 1983 GIA Publications. Used by permission.

248

Psalm 91

1. The— shel - ter of— the love— of God is my ref - uge
2. My— faith is in— the Lord— a - lone, his— Word my
3. Ev - er safe with - in— his love— I'll be se - cure through

and my light;— I— trust in him— to
help and shield.— When— thou - sands stum - ble
all my days.— The— won - der of— his

guide— my days and pro - tect me through— the night.—
by— my side, his— faith - ful - ness is re - vealed.—
might - y love al - ways fills my heart— with praise.—

Be - cause I come to him in love and trust him in all things, He an - swers when I call his name; he shel - ters me with his wings.

A Purple Robe

1. A pur-ple robe, a crown of thorn, a reed in his right
2. He hangs, by whom the world was made, be-neath the dark-ened

hand, Be - fore the sol - diers' spite and scorn I
sky; The ev - er - last - ing ran - som paid, I

see my Sav - ior stand. He bears be-tween the
see my Sav - ior die. He shares on high his

Ro - man guard the weight of all___ our woe;___ A
Fa - ther's throne who once in mer - cy came;___ For

stum - bling fig - ure bowed and scarred I see my Sav - ior go.___
all his love to sin - ners shown I sing my Sav - ior's name.___

Ready, Lord

Rejoice and Be Merry

1. Re - joice and be mer - ry in songs and in mirth! Oh, praise our Re - deem - er, all mor - tals on earth! For this is the birth - day of Je - sus our
2. A heav - en - ly vi - sion ap - peared in the sky; Vast num - bers of an - gels the shep - herds did spy, Pro - claim - ing the birth - day of Je - sus our
3. Like - wise a bright star in the sky did ap - pear, Which led the wise men from the East to draw near; They found the Mes - si - ah, sweet Je - sus our
4. And when they were come, they their treas - ures un - fold, And un - to him of - fered myrrh, in - cense, and gold. So bless - ed for - ev - er be Je - sus our

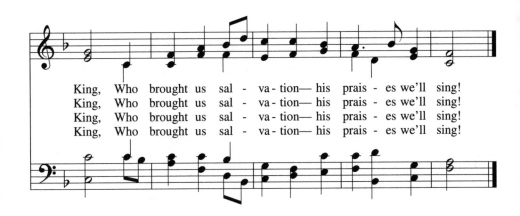

King, Who brought us sal - va - tion— his prais - es we'll sing!
King, Who brought us sal - va - tion— his prais - es we'll sing!
King, Who brought us sal - va - tion— his prais - es we'll sing!
King, Who brought us sal - va - tion— his prais - es we'll sing!

Text: traditional English carol. Tune: GALLERY CAROL. Setting: Reginald Jacques.
Setting: © 1961 Oxford University Press. Used by permission.

Jesus Loves Me
(Hmong translation)

Pronunciation:

1. Vajtswv hlub cov menyuam yaus
   Vajtswv phau ntawv qhia kuv paub
   Ntxhais thiab tub puavleej muaj nqe
   Yexu yeej tsis pub yuam kev

   Refrain
   Yexu hlub hlub kuv
   Yexu hlub hlub koj
   Yexu hlub hlub peb
   Vajtswv phau ntawv qhia kuv

2. Yexu hlub cov menyuam ntxhais
   Nws tsis pub ib tug ploj ntais
   Coj los nyob hauv nws xubntiag
   Pab lawv ua raw nws siab nyiam

   Refrain

3. Yexu hlub cov menyuam tub
   Lawv nyob zoo thiab kaj siab lug
   Pub kom muaj zog muaj siab tawv
   Pab tau ib tse neeg sawvdaws

   Refrain

1. vah-tsü hlü kô mA-nyüa yau
   vah-tsü p(h)au ntau khEa kü pau
   nts(h)I t(h)Ea tü püa-leng müa nkA
   yA-sü yeng tshE pü yüa kA

   Refrain
   yA-sü hlü hlü kü
   yA-sü hlü hlü kô
   yA-sü hlü hlü pA
   vah-tsü p(h)au ntau khEa kü

2. yA-sü hlü kô mA-nyüa nts(h)I
   nü tshE pü E tü plô ntI
   kô lô nyô hau nü sü-ntEa
   pa lau üa ja nü shla nyEa

   Refrain

3. yA-sü hlü kô mA-nyüa tü
   lau nyô zhông t(h)Ea ka shEa lü
   pü kô müa zhô müa shEa tau
   pa tau E tshA neng shô-dau

   Refrain

Pronunciation guide:
A, E, I = long vowels
ô = *ou* as in *cough*
ü = *oo* as in *zoo*
s(h) = *s* with breathy ending

Rejoice in the Lord Always

Re - joice in the Lord— al - ways, and a - gain I say, re - joice!

Re - joice in the Lord— al - ways, and a - gain I say, re - joice!

Re - joice, re - joice, and a - gain I say, re - joice!

Re - joice, re - joice, and a - gain I say, re - joice!

Tune: traditional. Setting: Dale Grotenhuis.
Setting: © 1987 CRC Publications. Used by permission.

Rescue the Perishing

1. Res - cue the per - ish - ing; care for the dy - ing;
2. Though they are slight - ing him, still he is wait - ing,
3. Down in the hu - man heart, crushed by the tempt - er,
4. Res - cue the per - ish - ing— du - ty de - mands it!

Snatch them in pit - y from sin and the grave.
Wait - ing the pen - i - tent child to re - ceive.
Feel - ings lie bur - ied that grace can re - store.
Strength for your la - bor the Lord will pro - vide.

Weep o'er the err - ing one; lift up the fall - en;
Plead with them ear - nest - ly; plead with them gent - ly;
Touched by a lov - ing heart, wak - ened by kind - ness,
Back to the nar - row way pa - tient - ly win them;

Tell them of Jesus, the mighty to save.
He will forgive if they only believe.
Chords that are broken will vibrate once more.
Tell the poor wand'rer a Savior has died.

Rescue the perishing; care for the dying.

Jesus is merciful; Jesus will save.

Text: Fanny J. Crosby. Tune and Setting: William H. Doane.

Rock of My Salvation

faith - ful love to me.—— You have been my help—— in

time of need;—— Lord, un - to you will I cleave.——

—— You are the rock—— of my——

—— sal - va - tion; You are the strength—— of my life.

Savior, like a Shepherd Lead Us

1. Sav - ior, like a shep - herd lead___ us;___ Much we
2. We are yours; in love be - friend___ us;___ Be the
3. Ev - er let us seek your fa - vor;___ Ev - er

need your ten - der care. In your pleas - ant pas - tures
guard - ian of our way. Keep your flock; from sin de -
let us do your will. Bless - ed Lord and on - ly

feed___ us;___ For our use your folds pre - pare.
fend___ us;___ Seek us when we go a - stray.
Sav - ior,___ With your love our hope ful - fill.

Bless - ed   Je - sus,   bless - ed   Je - sus,   You have
Bless - ed   Je - sus,   bless - ed   Je - sus,   Hear your
Bless - ed   Je - sus,   bless - ed   Je - sus,   You have

bought us;   yours   we   are.   Bless - ed   Je - sus,   bless - ed
chil - dren   when   they   pray.   Bless - ed   Je - sus,   bless - ed
loved   us;   love   us   still.   Bless - ed   Je - sus,   bless - ed

Je - sus,   You have   bought us;   yours   we   are.
Je - sus,   Hear your   chil - dren   when   they   pray.
Je - sus,   You have   loved   us;   love   us   still.

Text: attr. Dorothy A. Thrupp. Tune and Setting: William B. Bradbury.

Seek Ye First

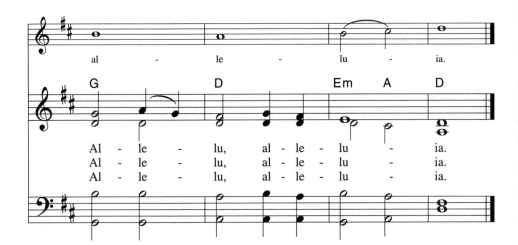

Tune and Setting: Karen Lafferty.

Text, Tune, Setting: © 1972 Maranatha! Music (administered by The Copyright Company, Nashville TN). All rights reserved. International Copyright Secured.
Used by permission.

She Will Be Called Blessed

Stanza 1: *spoken*
Her strength and her dignity clothe her with beauty;
In works of her hands she excels.
A heart of compassion she turns to the needy;
In service to others, she gives of herself.

Refrain

She will be called bless-ed By her sons and her daugh-ters;
Pre - cious to the Fa - ther Are those who seek his ways.
She will be called bless-ed, Help a - bove ev - 'ry oth - er;
Bless - ed is the moth - er Who turns to— God in praise.

Stanza 2: *spoken*
She rises each morning to see her household;
She looks toward the future with joy.
She teaches her children true lessons of kindness
And shares with them wisdom the world can't destroy.
Refrain

Text: Elizabeth deGravelles. Tune (IRENE) and Setting: Joseph Barlow.

Shine Down

Refrain

Shine down— your light— on me;— Let the peo - ple see— that in your pres - ence dark - ness flees.—

Fa - ther of light,— shine down— on me.—

Fa - ther of light,— shine down— on me.—

Fine

Verse

1. There's a land full of glo - ry
2. There's no sun in that cit - y;

In a place where there is— no night;—
The Fa - ther's throne is its on - ly light,—

And in that ho - ly cit - y
The lamp of sal - va - tion,

Burns the bea - con of ev - er - last - ing light,—
The hope that is al - ways glow - ing bright.—

The light that keeps reach - ing To the peo - ple of ev -
It scat - ters the dark - ness, Swept a - way by his might-

-'ry land,____ A love that is long-
-y hand;____ Now all the na-tions can wor-

-ing To fill the heart____ of ev-
-ship, Sing the song of that glo-

D.C.

-'ry-one.____
-rious____ Lamb.____

Text, Tune, Setting: Billy Smiley, Bob Farrell, and Mark Gersmehl.

Shine, Jesus, Shine

272

Flood the na - tions with grace and mer - cy.
Send forth your Word,___ Lord, And let there be

last time

light!

Text, Tune, Setting: Graham Kendrick.
Text, Tune, Setting: © 1987 Make Way Music. All rights reserved. International Copyright Secured.
Used by permission of Music Services.

Soon and Very Soon

1. Soon and ver - y soon,— We are going to see the King;—
2. No more dy - ing there,— We are going to see the King;—
3. No more cry - ing there,— We are going to see the King;—

Soon and ver - y soon,— We are going to see the King;—
No more dy - ing there,— We are going to see the King;—
No more cry - ing there,— We are going to see the King;—

Soon and ver - y soon,— We are going to see the King.—
No more dy - ing there,— We are going to see the King.—
No more cry - ing there,— We are going to see the King.—

Hal - le - lu - jah!— Hal - le - lu - jah!— We're going to see the King.—
Hal - le - lu - jah!— Hal - le - lu - jah!— We're going to see the King.—
Hal - le - lu - jah!— Hal - le - lu - jah!— We're going to see the King.—

Text and Tune: Andraé Crouch. Setting: William F. Smith.

The Snow Lay on the Ground

Text: traditional Christmas carol. Tune: VENITE ADOREMUS. Descant: Leo Sowerby.
Setting and Descant: © 1952 H. W. Gray Co. (administered by Warner Bros. Communications). Used by permission.

Softly and Tenderly

1. Soft - ly and ten - der - ly Je - sus is call - ing,
2. Why should we tar - ry when Je - sus is plead - ing,
3. Time is now fleet - ing, the mo - ments are pass - ing,
4. Oh, for the won - der - ful love he has prom - ised,

Call - ing for you and for me;
Plead - ing for you and for me?
Pass - ing from you and from me;
Prom - ised for you and for me;

See, on the por - tals he's wait - ing and watch - ing,
Why should we lin - ger and heed not his mer - cies,
Shad - ows are gath - er - ing, death-beds are com - ing,
Though we have sinned he has mer - cy and par - don,

Watch - ing for you and for me.____
Mer - cies for you and for me?____
Com - ing for you and for me.____
Par - don for you and for me.____

Come

home,____ come home,____ You who are wear-y, come

come home, come home,

home;____ Ear - nest-ly, ten - der - ly,

Je - sus is call-ing— Call-ing, "O sin - ner, come home!"____

Text, Tune, Setting: Will L. Thompson.

Some Children See Him

1. Some chil - dren see him lil - y—— white, The
2. Some chil - dren see him al - mond - eyed, This
3. The chil - dren in each dif - f'rent—— place Will

ba - by Je - sus—— born this night; Some chil - dren see him
Sav - ior whom we—— kneel be - side; Some chil - dren see him
see the ba - by—— Je - sus' face Like theirs, but bright with

lil - y—— white, With tress - es soft and—— fair. Some
al - mond - eyed, With skin of yel - low—— hue. Some
heav'n - ly—— grace And filled with ho - ly—— light. Oh,

279

children see him bronzed and brown, The
children see him dark as they, Sweet
lay a - side each earth - ly thing, And

Lord of heav'n to earth come down; Some children see him
Mar - y's Son, to whom we pray; Some children see him
with your heart as of - fer - ing, Come wor - ship now the

bronzed and brown, With dark and heav - y hair.
dark as they, And ah, they love him too!
in - fant King. 'Tis love that's born to - night!

Text: Wihla Hutson. Tune and Setting: Alfred S. Burt.

Somebody's Knocking at Your Door

Knocks like— Je - sus. Some-bod - y's knock-ing at your door.
Can't you— hear him? Some-bod - y's knock-ing at your door.
An - swer— Je - sus. Some-bod - y's knock-ing at your door.
Je - sus— calls you. Some-bod - y's knock-ing at your door.
Can't you— trust him? Some-bod - y's knock-ing at your door.

O———— sin - ner, why don't you an - swer?

Some-bod - y's knock-ing at your door.———

Text and Tune: African-American spiritual. Setting: Richard Proulx.
Setting: © 1986 GIA Publications. Used by permission.

Someone Special

1. Some - one spe - cial, I know who. That some - one, my
2. Some - one spe - cial, that you are, To cre - ate the
3. Some - one spe - cial, who would give His own Son that
4. Some - one spe - cial, who would send His good Spir - it
5. Some - one spe - cial— God and man— You were there when

God, is you, Who could make a world like this
Christ - mas star, Her - ald - ing the Sav - ior's birth,
all might live And by him would set us free
for a friend, Faith cre - a - tor, light, and guide,
I be - gan. You'll be there when I de - part,

And a heav - en full of bliss. Some - one spe - cial
Bring - ing peace and joy to earth. Some - one spe - cial
From all sin and mis - er - y. Some - one spe - cial
Al - ways stand - ing at my side. Some - one spe - cial
For you live with - in my heart. Some - one spe - cial—

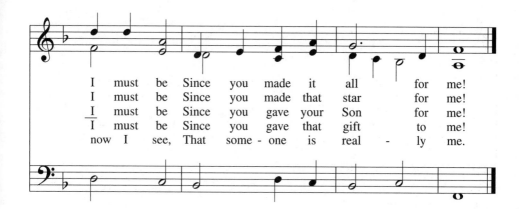

I   must   be   Since   you   made   it   all   for   me!
I   must   be   Since   you   made   that   star   for   me!
I   must   be   Since   you   gave   your   Son   for   me!
I   must   be   Since   you   gave   that   gift   to   me!
now   I   see,   That   some - one   is   real   -   ly   me.

Text: Jaroslav J. Vajda. Tune and Setting: Carl Schalk.
Text: © 1978 Jaroslav J. Vajda. Used by permission. Tune and Setting: © 1970 GIA Publications. Used by permission.

The Spirit of the Lord

The Spir-it of the Lord Fills all the world.___ The

Spir-it of the Lord Fills all the world.___ The Spir-it of the Lord___

Fills your love-ly world, O Lord. Al - le - lu - ia!

Let the right-eous be glad; Let them re-joice be-fore the Lord. Let the

right-eous be glad; Let them ex-ceed-ing-ly re-joice. The

Let God a-rise; Let his en-e-mies be scat-tered. Let God a-rise; Let his

en-e-mies be scat-tered. Let them that hate him al-so flee be-fore him,

Flee be-fore him, flee be-fore him, flee be-fore___ him. The

Standing on the Promises

1. Stand - ing on the prom - is - es of Christ my King,
2. Stand - ing on the prom - is - es that can - not fail
3. Stand - ing on the prom - is - es of Christ the Lord,
4. Stand - ing on the prom - is - es I can - not fall,

Through e - ter - nal a - ges let his prais - es ring;
When the howl - ing storms of doubt and fear as - sail,
Bound to him e - ter - nal - ly by love's strong cord,
Lis - t'ning ev - 'ry mo - ment to the Spir - it's call,

Glo - ry in the high - est, I will shout and sing,
By the liv - ing Word of God I shall pre - vail,
O - ver - com - ing dai - ly with the Spir - it's sword,
Rest - ing in my Sav - ior as my all in all,

Standing on the promises of God.
Standing on the promises of God.
Standing on the promises of God.
Standing on the promises of God.

standing,
Standing, standing on the promises, Standing on the promises of

standing, I'm
God my Savior; Standing, standing on the promises, I'm

standing on the promises of God.

Text, Tune, Setting: R. Kelso Carter.

Steal Away

Refrain

Steal a-way, steal a-way, steal a-way to Je - sus!

Steal a-way, steal a-way home, I ain't got long to stay here!

Verse

1. My Lord, he calls me, He calls me by the thun - der.
2. Green trees are bend - ing, Poor sin - ner stands a - trem - bling.
3. My Lord, he calls me, He calls me by the light - ning.
4. My Lord, he calls me, He calls me by the thun - der.

1., 2., 3., 4. The trum - pet sounds with - in - a my soul; I ain't got long to stay here.

Text and Tune: African-American spiritual.

Still, Still, Still

1. Still, still, still, Your heart with joy I'd fill. I'd sing you a song and watch by your man-ger, Guard you from harm and keep you from dan-ger. Still, still, still, Your heart with joy I'd fill.

2. Sleep, sleep, sleep, 'Mid the ox-en and the sheep. The shep-herds come to see your glo-ry; An-gels bend low to tell the sto-ry. Sleep, sleep, sleep, 'Mid the ox-en and the sheep.

3. Still, still, still, With-in your ho-ly will. To you, great God, my voice I'll raise, With awe and won-der sing your praise. Still, still, still, With-in your ho-ly will.

Text: Austrian carol; tr. George K. Evans. Tune: Austrian carol. Setting: Walter Ehret.
Text and Setting: from *The International Book of Christmas Carols* © 1963, 1980 Walter Ehret and George K. Evans. Used by permission.

Swing Low, Sweet Chariot

Refrain

Swing low, sweet char - i- ot,—— Com- ing for to car- ry me home;

Swing—— low,—— sweet char - i- ot,—— Com- ing for to car- ry me home.

Verse

1. I looked o - ver Jor - dan, and what did I see,——
2. If you get—— there be - fore—— I do,——
3. Some- times I'm—— up, some - times—— I'm down,——

Com-ing for to car-ry me home? A band— of an - gels
Com-ing for to car-ry me home, Tell all— my friends I'm
Com-ing for to car-ry me home, But still— I know I'm

com - ing af - ter me,— Com-ing for to car-ry me home.
com - ing there— too,— Com-ing for to car-ry me home.
heav - en - ward— bound,— Com-ing for to car-ry me home.

Text and Tune: African-American spiritual.

Tender Lord, by Your Word

Verse

1. Each night, my head on my pil - low,_____
2. Je - sus, my strength and my for - tress,_____
3. When I'm a - shamed in my con - science_____
4. Praise al - ways be to the Fa - ther,_____

Dark - ness and fear come to me._____
Ten - der - ly watch - es o'er me,_____
For all the wrong I have done,_____
Praise al - ways be to the Son,_____

Je - sus knows how to dis - miss them_____
Guid - ing my life through my trou - bles_____
Je - sus will cleanse me and cure me_____
Glo - ry to you, Ho - ly Spir - it,_____

With his love._____
With his Word._____
With his blood._____
Three in One._____

Text and Tune: Kenneth Kremer. Setting: Carl Nolte.
Text and Tune: © 1980 Kenneth Kremer. Used by permission. Setting: © 1998 Northwestern Publishing House.

Thanks Be to God

1. Thanks be to God, oh, give him praise And pub - li - cize his
2. Glo - ri - ous is his ho - ly name; Let ev - 'ry heart be
3. He sure - ly is our God and Lord, Who all the earth rules
4. God of cre - a - tion, Fa - ther blest; And Je - sus Christ our

great name. Shout out, pro - claim a - loud his
joy - ful. Cleansed they be - come through fear in
just - ly. His cov - 'nant he will not for -
Sav - ior; Spir - it of truth, our strength and

deeds To ev - 'ry land and peo - ple! Sing songs of
faith Who strug - gle now with cour - age. Look to the
get; It is his word and prom - ise. Each gen - er -
pow'r, Who calls us through the gos - pel— O tri - une

beau - ty to the Lord; Praise him with spir - it
Lord and to his strength; His acts re - call, his
a - tion this con - firms: He is un - fail - ing,
God, great Three in One, All a - ges glo - ri -

ju - bi - lant. Tell o - ver all his____ mar - vels!
judg - ments sound. Nev - er for - get his____ won - ders!
faith - ful, true; His trust is ev - er - last - ing.
fy your name Now and for - ev - er.____ A - men!

Text: Cornelius Becker; tr. Daniel G. Reuning. Tune (DANKET DEM HERREN): Heinrich Schutz.
Text: tr. © 1972 GIA Publications. Used by permission.

There Is a Green Hill Far Away

1. There is a green hill far a - way, Out - side a cit - y wall, Where the dear Lord was cru - ci - fied, Who died to save us all.
2. We may not know, we can - not tell, What pains he had to bear, But we be - lieve it was for us He hung and suf - fered there.
3. He died that we might be for - giv'n, He died to make us good, That we might go at last to heav'n, Saved by his pre - cious blood.
4. There was no oth - er good e - nough To pay the price of sin. He on - ly could un - lock the gate Of heav'n and let us in.

Text: Cecil F. Alexander, alt. Tune and Setting: William Horsley.

These Things Did Thomas Count

1. These things did Thom - as count as real:
2. The vi - sion of his skep - tic mind
3. His rea - soned cer - tain - ties de - nied
4. May we, O God, by grace be - lieve

The warmth of blood, the chill of steel,
Was keen e - nough to make him blind
That one could live when one had died,
And thus the ris - en Christ re - ceive,

The grain of wood, the heft of stone,
To an - y un - ex - pect - ed act
Un - til his fin - gers read like braille
Whose raw, im - print - ed palms reached out

The last frail twitch of flesh and bone.
Too large for his small world of fact.
The mark - ings of the spear and nail.
And beck - oned Thom - as from his doubt.

Text: Thomas H. Troeger. Tune: Carol Doran.
Text, Tune, Setting: from *New Songs for the Lectionary* © 1984 Oxford University Press. Used by permission.

They'll Know We Are Christians by Our Love

1. We are one in the Spir - it, we are one in the
2. We will walk with each oth - er, we will walk hand in
3. We will work with each oth - er, we will work side by
4. All___ praise to the Fa - ther, from whom all things___

Lord, We are one in the Spir - it, we are
hand, We will walk with each oth - er, we will
side, We will work with each oth - er, we will
come, And all praise to Christ Je - sus, his___

one in the Lord, And we pray that all
walk hand in hand, And to - geth - er we'll
work side by side. We'll re - spect peo - ple's
on - ly___ Son, And all praise to the

u - ni - ty may one day be re - stored.
spread the news that God is in our land.
dig - ni - ty and in love a - bide.
Spir - it, who makes us one.

And they'll know we are Chris-tians by our love, by our

love; Yes, they'll know we are Chris-tians by our love.

Text, Tune, Setting: Peter Scholtes.

This Is He

1. In a low - ly—— man - ger born, Hum - ble life be -
2. Vis - it - ing the—— lone and lost, Stead - y - ing the
3. Then, to res - cue—— you and me, Je - sus died up -

gun in scorn, Un - der Jo - seph's watch - ful eye,
tem - pest - tossed, Giv - ing of him - self in love,
on the tree. See in him God's love re - vealed;

Je - sus grew as you and I; Knew the suf - f'rings
Call - ing minds to things a - bove. Sin - ners glad - ly
By his pas - sion we are healed. Now he lives in

of the weak, Knew the pa - tience of the meek,——
hear his call, Pen - i - tent, be - fore him fall,——
glo - ry bright, Lives a - gain in pow'r and might;——

Hun - gered as but poor folk can.
For in him new life be - gan.
Come and take the path he trod—

This is he; be - hold the man!
This is he; be - hold the man!
Son of Mar - y, Son of God.

This Is My Father's World

1. This —— is my Fa - ther's world, And ——
2. This —— is my Fa - ther's world. The ——
3. This —— is my Fa - ther's world. Oh, ——

to my lis - t'ning ears, All na - ture sings and ——
birds their car - ols raise; The morn - ing light, the ——
let me ne'er for - get That though the wrong seems ——

'round me rings; His grace —— to me ap -
lil - y white, De - clare —— their Mak - er's ——
oft so strong, God is —— the rul - er ——

pears. This is my Fa - ther's world. I____
praise. This is my Fa - ther's world. He____
yet. This is my Fa - ther's world. Why____

rest me in the thought Of rocks and trees, of____
shines in all that's fair. In rus - tling grass I____
should my heart be sad? The Lord is King; let the

skies and seas; His hands____ these won - ders____ wrought.
hear him pass; I see____ his hand ev - 'ry - where.
heav - ens ring. God reigns;____ let earth be____ glad!

Text: Maltbie Davenport Babcock. Tune (TERRA PATRIS) and Setting: Franklin Lawrence Sheppard.

This Is the Day
(Sleeth)

Refrain

This is the day that the Lord— has— made! Re-
joice! Re - joice and be ex - ceed - ing glad!
This is the day that the Lord— has— made! Re-
joice! Re - joice! Hal - le - lu - jah!

1. Christ has con-quered death at last,
Left the tomb that held him fast!
Gone the sor-row, gone the night;
Dawns the morn-ing clear and bright!

2. Je-sus lives who once was dead,
Crown of glo-ry on his head!
Ris-en now our Lord and King;
Songs of glad-ness let us sing.

Text, Tune, Setting: Natalie Sleeth.
© 1977 Hinshaw Music. Used by permission.

This Is the Day
(Garrett)

This is—— the day, This is—— the day that the
Lord has made, That the Lord has made.
We will—— re - joice, We will—— re - joice and be
glad in it, And be glad in it.

This Is the Day When Light Was First Created

1. This is the—— day when light was first—— cre - a - ted,
2. This is the—— day of our com - plete—— sur - pris - ing,
3. This is the—— day of wor - ship and—— of—— vi - sion,
4. We pray that—— this, the day of re - cre - a - tion,

Sym - bol and—— gift of or - der and—— de - sign.
Re - peat of—— Eas - ter: Christ has come—— to life!
Great birth - day—— of the church in ev - 'ry land.
May hal - low—— all the week that is—— to come.

In light is—— God's in - ten - tion clear - ly—— stat - ed;
Now is the—— feast of love's re - volt—— and—— ris - ing
Let Chris - tians—— all con - fess their sad—— di - vi - sion
Help us, O—— Lord, to lay a good—— foun - da - tion

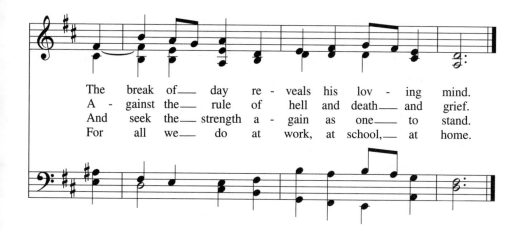

The   break of___ day   re - veals his   lov - ing   mind.
A -   gainst the___ rule   of   hell   and death___ and grief.
And   seek   the___ strength a - gain   as   one___   to stand.
For   all   we___   do   at   work, at school,___ at home.

Thy Holy Wings, O Savior

1. Thy— ho - ly wings, O— Sav - ior, Spread— gent - ly o - ver me, And— let me rest se - cure - ly Through good and ill in thee. Oh,— be my strength and— por - tion, My

2. Oh,— wash me in the— wa - ters Of— No - ah's cleans - ing flood; Give— me a will - ing— spir - it, A— heart both clean and good. And— take in - to thy— keep - ing Thy

rock and hid - ing place, And__ let my ev - 'ry__
chil - dren great and small, And__ while we sweet - ly__

mo - ment Be__ lived with - in thy grace.
slum - ber, En - fold us one and all.

Text: Caroline V. Sandell-Berg; tr. Gracia Grindal. Tune: Swedish folk song. Setting: Lahrae Knatterud.
Text: tr © 1983 Gracia Grindal. Used by permission. Setting: © Lahrae Knatterud. Used by permission.

This Touch of Love

1. This touch of love,_____ this taste of peace,_____ _____ How can it last and still in-crease? I can-not bear_____ to have this air of won-der cease.
2. This hap-py feast,_____ this friend-ly bond,_____ _____ How can I keep it long be-yond This fleet-ing hour,_____ this surge of power, this treas-ure found?
3. Christ Je-sus, you_____ are what I need,_____ _____ The Bread and Wine on which I feed, No friend so true,_____ no life so new— I'm rich in-deed.
4. O Sav-ior, now_____ my spir-it raise._____ _____ Give new di-rec-tion to my ways, In all I view,_____ in all I do, to give you praise.

Text: Jaroslav J. Vajda. Tune and Setting: Carl F. Schalk.
Text: © 1987 Jaroslav J. Vajda. Used by permission. Tune and Setting: © 1987 GIA Publications. Used by permission.

Thy Word Is a Lamp

Thy Word is a lamp un-to my feet And a
light un-to my path.

last time to Coda

1. When I feel a-fraid, Think I've lost my way,
2. I will not for-get Your love for me, and yet My

Still you're there right be-side me. And
heart for-ev-er is wan-der-ing.

314

To Every Generation

Text and Tune: Bill Batstone.

Unto Us Is Born a Son

1. Un - to us is born a Son,
2. Christ, from heav'n des - cend - ing low,
3. Of his love and mer - cy mild—

King of choirs su - per - nal;
Comes on earth a stran - ger;
This the Christ - mas sto - ry;

See on earth his life be - gun, Of
Sheep and ox their own - er know, Be -
And that Mar - y's gen - tle child Might

lords the Lord e - ter - nal, Of
cra - dled in the man - ger, Be -
lead us up to glo - ry, Might

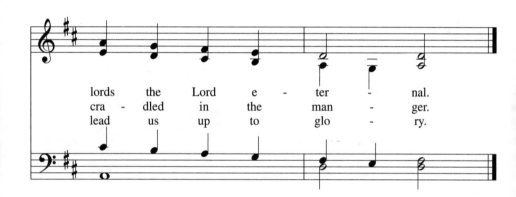

lords the Lord e - ter - nal.
cra - dled in the man - ger.
lead us up to glo - ry.

Text: from *Piae Cantiones;* tr. G. R. Woodward. Tune: from *Piae Cantiones.* Setting: David Willcocks.
Text: used by permission of Mowbray (a div. of Cassell plc). Setting: from *Carols for Choirs Book 1* © 1961 Oxford University Press. Used by permission.

We See the Lord

We Walk by Faith

1. We walk by faith and not by sight; No
2. We may not touch his hands and side Nor
3. Help then, O Lord, our un - be - lief, And
4. That when our life of faith is done In
5. We walk by faith and not by sight; No

sound or voice we hear_____ Of
fol - low where he trod,_____ Yet
may our faith a - bound_____ To
realms of clear - er light,_____ We
sound or voice we hear_____ Of

him who spoke as none e'er spoke, But
in his prom - ise we re - joice And
call on you when you are near And
may be - hold you as you are In
him who spoke as none e'er spoke, But

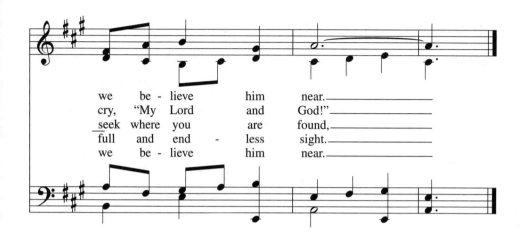

we   be - lieve   him   near.————————
cry,   "My   Lord   and   God!"————————
seek   where   you   are   found,————————
full   and   end - less   sight.————————
we   be - lieve   him   near.————————

Text: Henry Alford, alt. Tune (SHANTI) and Setting: Marty Haugen.
Tune and Setting: © 1985 GIA Publications. Used by permission.

We Will Glorify

1. We will glo - ri - fy the King of kings; We will glo - ri - fy the Lamb. We will glo - ri - fy the Lord of lords, Who___ is the great I AM.

2. Lord Je - ho - vah reigns in maj - es - ty; We will bow be - fore his throne. We will wor - ship him in right - eous - ness; We will wor - ship him a - lone.

3. He is Lord of heav - en, Lord of earth; He is Lord of all who live. He is Lord a - bove the u - ni - verse; All___ praise to him we give.

4. Hal - le - lu - jah to the King of kings; Hal - le - lu - jah to the Lamb. Hal - le - lu - jah to the Lord of lords, Who___ is the great I AM.

optional last stanza setting

4. Hal - le - lu - jah to the King of kings; Hal - le -
lu - jah to the Lamb. Hal - le - lu - jah to the
Lord of lords, Who— is the great I AM. Hal - le - AM.

Text and Tune: Twila Paris. Setting: David Allen.

We'll Understand It Better By and By

1. We are of-ten tossed and driv'n on the rest-less sea of time.
2. We are of-ten des-ti-tute of the things that life de-mands,
3. Tri-als dark on ev-'ry hand, and we can-not un-der-stand

Som-ber skies and howl-ing tem-pests oft suc-ceed a bright sun-shine.
Want of food and want of shel-ter, thirst-y hills and bar-ren lands.
All the ways that God would lead us to that bless-ed Prom-ised Land,

In that land of per-fect day, when the mists have rolled a-way,
We are trust-ing in the Lord, and ac-cord-ing to his Word,
But he guides us with his eye, and we'll fol-low till we die,
D.S.— how we've o-ver-come,

Fine

We will un - der - stand it bet - ter by and by.
We will un - der - stand it bet - ter by and by.
For we'll un - der - stand it bet - ter by and by.
For we'll un - der - stand it bet - ter by and by.

By and by when the morn - ing comes, When the saints of

D.S. al Fine

God are gath - ered home, We'll tell the sto - ry

Text and Tune: Charles Albert Tindley. Setting: F. A. Clark.

What Does the Lord Require

1. What does the Lord re - quire for praise and
2. Rul - ers of earth, give ear! Should you not
3. Still down the a - ges ring the proph - et's
4. How shall our life ful - fill God's law so

of - fer - ing, What sac - ri - fice, de -
jus - tice know? Will God your plead - ing
stern com - mands. To mer - chant, work - er,
hard and high? Let Christ en - due our

sire, or trib - ute bid you
hear while crime and cruel - ty
king, he brings God's high de -
will with grace to for - ti -

bring?   Do   just - ly;   love   mer - cy;   walk
grow?   Do   just - ly;   love   mer - cy;   walk
mands: Do   just - ly;   love   mer - cy;   walk
fy.   Then   just - ly,   in   mer - cy,   we'll

1., 2., 3.

4.

hum - bly   with   your   God.
hum - bly   with   your   God.
hum - bly   with   your   God.

hum - bly   walk   with   God.

Text: Albert F. Bayly, alt. Tune (SHARPTHORNE) and Setting: Erik Routley.

While by the Sheep

1. While by the sheep we watched at night,
2. There shall be born, so he did say,
3. There shall the child lie in a stall,
4. This gift of God we'll cher - ish well—

Glad tid - ings brought an an - gel bright.
In Beth - le - hem a child to - day.
This child who shall re - deem us all.
Je - sus, our Lord Im - man - u - el.

echo

How great our joy! Great our joy! Joy, joy, joy!

Joy, joy, joy! Praise we the Lord in heav'n on high! Praise we the Lord in heav'n on high!

Text: German carol; tr. Theodore Baker, alt. Tune (JUNGST) and Setting: Hugo Jungst.

Who Is He in Yonder Stall

'Tis the Lord! Oh, won-drous sto-ry! 'Tis the Lord, the King of glo-ry! At his feet we hum-bly fall. Crown him, crown him Lord of all!

Text and Tune: Benjamin R. Hanby.

Yes, He Did

I can tell the world a-bout this; I can tell the na-tions I'm blest,——— Tell them that Je - sus made me whole. He brought joy to my soul!

Text: traditional. Tune: African-American spiritual. Setting: Carl Nolte.
Setting: © 1998 Northwestern Publishing House.

You Have Made Us One

1. Be - cause you loved us first, O Lord,
2. The joy that shouts from deep with - in
3. Join our hands a - round the cross;

In your ho - ly Son, We know your love has
Can - not be con - tained. We know that in this
Fold them close in prayer. And when we look be -

brought us here; You have made us one.
love you sent, We will now re - main.
yond that cross, We will see you there.

Take our love, O Lord, and make it right;
Shine it in the fear - ful night. We be-lieve with
all our might: You have made us one!

The Word

1. The Word is liv-ing; The Word is light. The Word de-
2. The Word is wis-dom; The Word is true. The Word takes
3. The Word is call-ing Time and a-gain; The Word is

lights my soul, Pre-serves my life. Ho - ly and
all that's old And makes it new. When hearts are
griev-ing still For those in sin. Come now be-

hid-den, For-ev-er new, The per-fect
bro-ken, He makes them whole. The one who
liev-ing His Word is true. The cross speaks

sac-ri-fice: Our Lord Je-sus Christ.
paid the price: Our Lord Je-sus Christ.
this ad-vice: "Trust me, Je-sus Christ."

Copyright Holders and Administrators

Permission to reproduce any copyrighted words or music contained in this book must be obtained from the copyright holder(s) of that material. For addresses of copyright holders not listed below, please contact Northwestern Publishing House.

AUGSBURG FORTRESS
100 S Fifth St Suite 700
Minneapolis MN 55440-1209
1-800-421-0239
Fax (612) 330-3252

BMG MUSIC PUBLISHERS
1400 18th Ave S
Nashville TN 37212
(615) 858-1332
Fax (615) 858-1330

BOURNE COMPANY MUSIC PUBLISHERS
5 W 37th St
New York NY 10018
(212) 391-4300
Fax (212) 391-4306

BREITKOPF & HÄRTEL
Walkmülstrasse 52
Postfach 1707
D-65195 Wiesbaden 1 Germany
011-611-45008-0
Fax 011-611-45008-59

BRENTWOOD-BENSON MUSIC PUBLISHING
741 Cool Springs Blvd
Nashville TN 37067-2697
(615) 261-3337
Fax (615) 261-3386

CASSELL PLC
Wellington House
125 Strand
London WC2R 0BB England
011-44-171-420-5555
Fax 011-44-171-240-7261

CHANGING CHURCH FORUM
200 E Nicollet Blvd
Burnsville MN 55337

CHORISTERS GUILD
2834 W Kingsley Rd
Garland TX 75041-2498
(972) 271-1521
Fax (972) 840-3113

CHURCH OF THE MESSIAH
231 E Grand Blvd
Detroit MI 48207-3788

CONCORDIA PUBLISHING HOUSE
3558 S Jefferson Ave
Saint Louis MO 63118
1-800-325-3391
Fax (314) 268-1329

THE COPYRIGHT COMPANY
40 Music Square E
Nashville TN 37203
(615) 244-5588
Fax (615) 244-5591

CRC PUBLICATIONS
2850 Kalamazoo SE
Grand Rapids MI 49560
1-800-333-8300
Fax (616) 224-0834

EMI CHRISTIAN MUSIC PUBLISHERS
101 Winners Circle
Brentwood TN 37024-5085
(615) 371-6880
Fax (615) 371-6897

THE EVANGELICAL COVENANT CHURCH
5101 N Francisco Ave
Chicago IL 60625-3611

FAIRHILL MUSIC
PO Box 4467
Oceanside CA 92052
(760) 806-3672
Fax (760) 806-3673

GIA PUBLICATIONS INC
7404 S Mason Ave
Chicago IL 60638
(708) 496-3800
Fax (708) 496-3828

HAL LEONARD PUBLISHING CORPORATION
7777 W Bluemound Rd PO Box 13819
Milwaukee WI 53213
(414) 774-3630
Fax (414) 774-3259

HINSHAW MUSIC INC
PO Box 470
Chapel Hill NC 27514-0470
(919) 933-1691
Fax (919) 967-3399

HOPE PUBLISHING COMPANY
380 S Main Pl
Carol Stream IL 60188
1-800-323-1049
Fax (630) 665-2552

INTEGRITY MUSIC INC
1000 Cody Rd
Mobile AL 36695-3425
(334) 633-9000
Fax (334) 633-9998

Copyright Holders and Administrators

THE LORENZ CORPORATION
501 E Third St
Dayton OH 45401-0802
1-800-444-1144
Fax (937) 223-2042

THE LUTHERAN WORLD FEDERATION
PO Box 2100
Route de Ferney 150
CH-1211 Geneva 2, Switzerland
011-41-22-791-61-11
Fax 011-41-22-798-86-16

MANNA MUSIC INC
35255 Brooten Rd
PO Box 218
Pacific City OR 97135
(503) 965-6112
Fax (503) 965-6880

EDWARD B MARKS MUSIC COMPANY
c/o Carlin America, Inc
126 E 38th St
New York NY 10016
(212) 779-7977
Fax (212) 779-7920

KEVIN MAYHEW LTD
Rattlesden Bury
St. Edmunds
Suffolk 1P30 OSZ UK
Fax 011-441-449-737-834

MCCRIMMON PUBLISHERS
10-12 High Street
Great Wakening Southend-on-the-Sea
Essex UK 553 OEQ

MUSIC SALES CORPORATION
257 Park Ave S
New York NY 10010
(212) 254-2100
Fax (212) 254-2013

MUSIC SERVICES
209 Chapelwood Dr
Franklin TN 37069
(615) 794-9015
Fax (615) 794-0793

OCP PUBLICATIONS
5536 NE Hassalo
Portland OR 97212-3638
(503) 281-1191
Fax (503) 282-3486

OXFORD UNIVERSITY PRESS
Great Clarendon St
Oxford OX 2 6DP England
011-44-1865-556-767
Fax 011-44-1865-267-749

THE RICHMOND ORGANIZATION (TRO)
11 W 19th St
New York NY 10011
(212) 627-4646
Fax (212) 633-1233

SAVGOS MUSIC INC
1012 18th Ave S
Nashville TN 37212
Fax (615) 329-3964

TRUST MUSIC MANAGEMENT
PO Box 22274
Carmel CA 93922
(831) 626-1030
Fax (831) 626-1026

WALTON MUSIC CORPORATION
PO Box 167
Bynum NC 27228
(919) 542-5548
Fax (919) 542-5527

WARNER BROS PUBLICATIONS
15800 NW 48th Ave PO Box 4340
Miami FL 33014
(305) 620-1500
Fax (305) 625-3480

WESTMINSTER/JOHN KNOX PRESS
100 Witherspoon St
Louisville KY 40202-1396
1-800-523-1631

WORD MUSIC INC
PO Box 128469
Nashville TN 37212-8469
(615) 385-9673
Fax (615) 457-1960

JOHN YLVISAKER/
NEW GENERATIONS PUBLISHERS
Box 321
Waverly IA 50677
(319) 352-3814

First Lines and Common Titles

First Lines and Common Titles